WORLD
HISTORY SERIES ■ ■ ■

The American Frontier

Titles in the World History Series

The American Frontier

by
Roger Barr

Lucent Books, P.O. Box 289011, San Diego, CA 92198-9011

_JH/J_

Library of Congress Cataloging-in-Publication Data

Barr, Roger, 1951–
    The American frontier / by Roger Barr
       p. cm.—(World history series)
    Includes bibliographical references and index.
    Summary: Examines the history of the formative years of
the United States, focusing on westward expansion and the
role of the frontier in shaping the new nation.
    ISBN 1-56006-282-7 (alk. paper)
    1. United States—Territorial expansion—Juvenile litera-
ture. 2. Frontier and pioneer life—United States—Juvenile literature. 3. Frontier thesis—Juvenile literature. [1. United
States—Territorial expansion. 2. Frontier and pioneer life.]
I.Title. II. Series.
E179.5.B37   1996
974.4'5—dc20   95-38312
                                        CIP
                                        AC

Copyright 1996 by Lucent Books, Inc., P.O. Box 289011,
San Diego, California, 92198-9011

Printed in the U.S.A.

16.95

Contents

Foreword

Each year on the first day of school, nearly every history teacher faces the task of explaining why his or her students should study history. One logical answer to this question is that exploring what happened in our past explains how the things we often take for granted—our customs, ideas, and institutions—came to be. As statesman and historian Winston Churchill put it, "Every nation or group of nations has its own tale to tell. Knowledge of the trials and struggles is necessary to all who would comprehend the problems, perils, challenges, and opportunities which confront us today." Thus, a study of history puts modern ideas and institutions in perspective. For example, though the founders of the United States were talented and creative thinkers, they clearly did not invent the concept of democracy. Instead, they adapted some democratic ideas that had originated in ancient Greece and with which the Romans, the British, and others had experimented. An exploration of these cultures, then, reveals their very real connection to us through institutions that continue to shape our daily lives.

Another reason often given for studying history is the idea that lessons exist in the past from which contemporary societies can benefit and learn. This idea, although controversial, has always been an intriguing one for historians. Those that agree that society can benefit from the past often quote philosopher George Santayana's famous statement, "Those who cannot remember the past are condemned to repeat it." Historians who ascribe to Santayana's philosophy believe that, for example, studying the events that led up to the major world wars or other significant historical events would allow society to chart a different and more favorable course in the future.

Just as difficult as convincing students to realize the importance of studying history is the search for useful and interesting supplementary materials that present historical events in a context that can be easily understood. The volumes in Lucent Books' World History Series attempt to present a broad, balanced, and penetrating view of the march of history. Ancient Egypt's important wars and rulers, for example, are presented against the rich and colorful backdrop of Egyptian religious, social, and cultural developments. The series engages the reader by enhancing historical events with these cultural contexts. For example, in *Ancient Greece*, the text covers the role of women in that society. Slavery is discussed in *The Roman Empire*, as well as how slaves earned their freedom. The numerous and varied aspects of everyday life in these and other societies are explored in each volume of the series. Additionally, the series covers the major political, cultural, and philosophical ideas as the torch of civilization is passed from ancient Mesopotamia and Egypt, through Greece, Rome, Medieval Europe, and other world cultures, to the modern day.

The material in the series is formatted in a thorough, precise, and organized manner. Each volume offers the reader a comprehensive and clearly written overview of an important historical event or period. The topic under discussion is placed in a broad historical context. For example, *The Italian Renaissance* begins with a discussion of the High Middle Ages and the loss of central control that allowed certain Italian cities to develop artistically. The book ends by looking forward to the Reformation and interpreting the societal changes that grew out of the Renaissance. Thus, students are not only involved in an historical era, but also enveloped by the events leading up to that era and the events following it.

One important and unique feature in the World History Series is the primary and secondary source quotations that richly supplement each volume. These quotes are useful in a number of ways. First, they allow students access to sources they would not normally be exposed to because of the difficulty and obscurity of the original source. The quotations range from interesting anecdotes to far-sighted cultural perspectives and are drawn from historical witnesses both past and present. Second, the quotes demonstrate how and where historians themselves derive their information on the past as they strive to reach a consensus on historical events. Lastly, all of the quotes are footnoted, familiarizing students with the citation process and allowing them to verify quotes and/or look up the original source if the quote piques their interest.

Finally, the books in the World History Series provide a detailed launching point for further research. Each book contains a bibliography specifically geared toward student research. A second, annotated bibliography introduces students to all the sources the author consulted when compiling the book. A chronology of important dates gives students an overview, at a glance, of the topic covered. Where applicable, a glossary of terms is included.

In short, the series is designed not only to acquaint readers with the basics of history, but also to make them aware that their lives are a part of an ongoing human saga. Perhaps they will then come to the same realization as famed historian Arnold Toynbee. In his monumental work, *A Study of History*, he wrote about becoming aware of history flowing through him in a mighty current and of his own life "welling like a wave in the flow of this vast tide."

Important Dates in the History of the American Frontier

1492	1550	1600	1650	1700	1750	1800	1850	1900	1950	1960

1492
Christopher Columbus's visit to New World helps inaugurate an age of exploration.

1607
The first permanent English settlement in the New World is founded in Jamestown, Virginia.

1783
Treaty with Britain establishes independence of American colonies.

1785
Congress passes Ordinance of 1785, which establishes surveying procedures for U.S. public domain.

1787
Congress passes Ordinance of 1787, which establishes procedures for adding new states to the Union.

1803
Louisiana Purchase completed, doubling the size of the United States.

1819
Florida ceded by Spain to United States.

1820
Missouri Compromise forbids slavery north of Missouri's southern border.

1846
Texas annexed by United States, increasing its size by 250,000 square miles; treaty with Britain establishing 49th parallel as boundary between U.S. and Canada gives much of Oregon territory to United States.

1848
In Treaty of Guadalupe Hidalgo, Mexico cedes New Mexico and California to United States, fulfilling America's "manifest destiny"; gold discovery in California touches off great westward migration.

1850
Congress passes Compromise of 1850, giving territories right to choose or reject slavery.

1853
James Gadsden purchases strip of land from Mexico for railroad, Gadsden

Purchase completes present continental borders of United States.

1854
Kansas-Nebraska Act repeals Missouri Compromise, setting stage for Civil War.

1890–93
In several Oklahoma land rushes, settlers claim last of America's land in the public domain.

1893
Frederick Jackson Turner presents his frontier hypothesis.

1912
New Mexico and Arizona admitted to Union, completing America's forty-eight contiguous states.

1960
Alaska and Hawaii admitted in 1960 as forty-ninth and fiftieth states, respectively; Democratic presidential candidate John F. Kennedy uses the phrase "new frontier" to describe the challenges Americans face in the future.

A Primary Force in American History

When early European explorers dropped anchor off North America's eastern coast and waded ashore in the early 1500s, they had no idea they were stepping onto a vast continent. To the west, beyond the tidelands, rose a great mountain range. Beyond the mountains stretched a thousand miles of fertile prairies, broad dusty plains, and burning deserts. Beyond the deserts rose another great mountain range filled with precious metals. Finally, three thousand miles from where the explorers stood on the Atlantic coast, was another great ocean that became known as the Pacific.

Nor could these early explorers know that their first steps onto the shore would initiate the many succeeding steps that would eventually create the United States

Stopping to pose for a photo in front of their covered wagon, a family pursues a frontier homestead. The settlement of the frontier played a significant part in the shaping of American culture.

of America. The explorers had crossed the turbulent Atlantic in search of adventure, opportunity, and riches. For the next four hundred years, these same desires would drive their descendants into the wilderness until at last they reached the Pacific. As members of each succeeding generation moved west to claim the land and shape it to fit their desires and needs, the land in turn helped to shape the nation they built and the values of the people themselves.

Many Frontiers

The concept that the continent itself had been the primary force in the development of America was first proposed in 1893 by a young historian named Frederick Jackson Turner. Turner divided the long westward march across the continent into a series of frontiers. In his analysis of the east-to-west settlement of the continent, Turner defined the frontier in many ways. Sometimes the frontier was an invisible line separating the wilderness from civilization. In other times, the frontier was the vast wilderness itself. Sometimes the frontier was a boundary line between the new nation and a neighboring nation. And at other times it was a barrier—physical, such as a mountain range, or cultural, such as hostile native inhabitants who resisted the settlers' advance. Often he referred to the frontier simply as "the west."

Regardless of how he defined it at any given period of history, Turner observed that the frontier was always perceived as a place where people could acquire new land and start over, a place filled with opportunities that promised advancement and certain wealth. The waves of settlement across the continent in pursuit of free land and prosperity, Turner believed, explained the development of American democracy and shaped the American character.

Turner's "frontier hypothesis" revolutionized the study of American history. Historians turned away from Europe to explain the origins of America's important institutions and unique characteristics. Although Turner's frontier hypothesis is no longer universally accepted, the American frontier continues to be recognized as an important force in shaping the nation.

Although its physical borders have been officially fixed for decades, the idea of the American frontier continues to be significant even today. As it has been throughout American history, the frontier is still idealized in songs, literature, television programs, and movies. Americans still exhibit many character traits, good and bad, that can be traced back to the frontier period. As long as there is a United States of America, its frontier past will remain an important influence on the nation's future.

1 Europe's Frontier

The North American continent has always been a frontier to the nations of Europe, a land filled with opportunity, promise, and riches. As feudal Europe awoke from the Middle Ages' nearly ten centuries of isolation and economic stagnation, the fifteenth century became the age of great exploration. Explorers representing many nations set out in search of ocean routes to the Far East, where they hoped to trade in spices, gems, tapestries, precious stones, and other treasures.

Between Europe and the Far East, however, was an undiscovered continent. Although not necessarily the first European explorer to see this new continent, Christopher Columbus is certainly the most famous. In 1492, Columbus, an Italian sailing for Spain, landed among a group of islands, now called the West Indies, located south of the present-day United States. Columbus never understood that he had landed in the New World and not the Far East, but it did not

Christopher Columbus plants the Spanish flag in the soil of the New World, an event that would eventually lead to the rush to open the Atlantic frontier.

take long for other explorers to identify the strange land as a previously unknown continent that might contain riches of its own. The rush to open the Atlantic frontier and exploit its opportunities had begun.

Many explorers followed Columbus, but only three nations—Spain, France, and England—were successful in establishing permanent claims in the New World. Colonists from each nation recognized different opportunities in America and used different methods to exploit the bounties of the new continent. The empire-building efforts of these nations and their descendants over the next four hundred years eventually transformed the entire continent.

Spanish Claims

Columbus's voyages marked the beginning of attempts by Spain to establish an empire in the New World. In 1513, Juan Ponce de León explored a large peninsula of land that he christened Florida in search of a magical spring whose waters were said to bestow eternal youth. Ponce de León never found his magical fountain, but his explorations furthered Spanish claims to the New World.

Spanish interests in the New World were primarily economic. Between 1513 and 1590, a succession of Spanish frontiersmen known as conquistadors explored the Gulf of Mexico in search of gold and silver. One of them, Hernando de Soto, arrived in the New World in 1538. Historian Ray Allen Billington describes de Soto's exploration of what is now the southeastern United States:

After wintering in Cuba, the elaborate force of six hundred soldiers, great herds of horses and swine, packs of hounds, and mountains of equipment landed on the east shore of Tampa Bay in May, 1539. There began four years of fruitless wandering over 350,000 square miles of wilderness, guided only by Indians who discovered that they could best rid themselves of the plundering Spaniards by telling them that the next village was richer than their own.[1]

When de Soto failed to find riches in the American interior, the Spanish stopped searching for gold and silver and focused on establishing a successful colony. In 1565, mariner Don Pedro Menéndes de Avilés established the settlement of St. Augustine on the Atlantic coastline of Florida, the first permanent European settlement in the New World. Spanish missionaries soon constructed a series of missions across the southern part of North America. The missionaries were successful in converting some natives to Christianity and the allegiance of the natives to the missions helped Spain secure its colonial interests. From this beginning, Spain established a presence across the southern part of the present United States that continued for more than three hundred years.

The Arrival of the French

The French first arrived in the New World forty years after Columbus. Like the Spanish, the French were primarily interested in exploiting the bounties of the New World. Instead of seeking gold and silver,

Jacques Cartier's ships ascend the St. Lawrence River, eager to exploit the riches of the New World.

The most influential French frontiersman was Samuel de Champlain. In June of 1608, Champlain founded the Canadian city of Quebec. With this settlement as his base, Champlain befriended native tribes and explored the continent's interior. His wanderings blazed trails that served as French highways into the interior for decades. The French empire in the New World endured for more than a century and a half.

Although the Spanish and French pursued different economic opportunities in the New World, they employed similar methods. Colonists from both nations

With the help of Native Americans, French frontiersman Samuel de Champlain carves out the beginnings of the French empire in the New World.

however, the French concentrated their efforts on fishing and trapping. In 1534, Jacques Cartier, sailing for the French king, explored the St. Lawrence River, venturing as far upstream as the site of present-day Montreal. Two attempts by Cartier to establish a colony failed. French fishermen proved more successful than Cartier, eventually dominating the fishing industry that developed off the coast of Newfoundland. By 1578, 150 French ships were fishing in the frigid waters of the North Atlantic, compared to a combined total of 50 from England, Holland, Spain, and Portugal.

French interests soon shifted from fishing to fur trading with the native inhabitants. Trading began along the coast, but eager Frenchmen soon began traveling up the St. Lawrence and other rivers to intercept the furs as they were transported to the coast.

sought to exploit the wilderness around them for the benefit of their king or company, but made little attempt to subdue, conquer, and own the land itself. In this respect, the French and Spanish attitude toward the land was compatible with that of the Native American nations who originally inhabited it. Although conflicts between French and Spanish colonists and natives were inevitable, in general they coexisted in relative harmony.

English Colonists

Although England was the last of the three nations to enter the race for riches in the New World, English colonization efforts proved the most successful. English colonists learned from their early mistakes and developed new frontiering techniques that were more successful than those of the French and Spanish colonists.

Like the French and Spanish, England pursued mainly economic goals in its earliest ventures into the New World. Sailing for Queen Elizabeth I, Sir Walter Raleigh sent three expeditions to the New World in 1584, 1585, and 1587. The first two expeditions returned to England without establishing a colony. The third settled on Roanoke Island off the coast of present-day Virginia and North Carolina, but before a supply ship arrived in 1591 to resupply the colony, the colonists disappeared without a trace.

Alone, Raleigh lacked the means necessary to sustain the colonists while they learned to sustain themselves in the New World. Cold winters, inability to grow European crops, and conflicts with Indians ultimately undermined Raleigh's efforts.

His failures taught the English that no one man was capable of establishing a colony. The combined resources of many people were necessary to make a colony succeed. This realization helped transform the New World into a land of opportunity for merchants and common people, instead of remaining the province of the wealthy.

Perhaps with this lesson in mind, a group known as the London Company began construction in 1607 of a settlement near what is known today as Chesapeake Bay. Jamestown, named in honor of the English king James I, became the first permanent English colony in the New World. During its first year, the colony nearly suffered the same fate Raleigh's had, as the settlers struggled to adapt to their new environment. Fortunately, Captain John Smith motivated the settlers to work

Under the leadership of Captain John Smith, Jamestown became the first permanent English colony in America.

Virginia's Claim

English colonist Captain John Smith began his Description of Virginia and proceedings of the Colonie, *published in 1612, with this passage. For nearly two centuries, Virginia's claim was extended from the Atlantic coast west to the Pacific Ocean. The quote was published in* Narratives of Early Virginia.

"Virginia is a Country in America, that lyeth betweene the degrees of 34 and 44 of the north latitude. The bounds thereof on the East side are the great Ocean. On the South lyeth Florida: on the North nova Francia. As for the West thereof, the limits are unknowne. Of all this country wee purpose not to speak, but only of that part which was planted by the English men in the yeare of our Lord, 1606. And this is under the degrees 37. 38. and 39. The temperature of this countrie doth agree well with English constitutions being once seasoned to the country. Which appeared by this, that though by many occasions our people fell sicke; yet did they recover by very small means and continued in health, though there were other great causes, not only to have made them sicke, but even to end their daies."

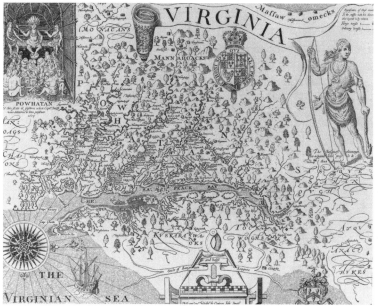

Smith's 1612 map of Virginia shows the locations of the Native American tribes that inhabited the area at the time.

together. Smith also secured grain from Native Americans for the colonists to plant. Under Smith's leadership, the colony survived. Within two years, the colonists began growing tobacco, which they exported to England.

The colony did not really begin to prosper, however, until London Company officials began dividing up the land into small parcels and transferring ownership of them to the colonists. For the first time, English colonists had the opportunity to own land. With a chance to increase their own wealth, colonists worked harder. The Virginia colony began to prosper.

In Search of Spiritual Fulfillment

At the same time that the Virginia colonists labored to establish a southern colony, a second English company began to grant tracts of land given to them by King James to small groups of settlers. The first group to purchase a tract was a band of religious dissenters who originally had fled England for Holland. To the 102 colonists who set sail aboard the *Mayflower* in 1620, America offered spiritual fulfillment. To these colonists, who became known as Pilgrims, America represented the opportunity to worship as they pleased, without fear of persecution.

Before the ship reached its intended goal of Virginia, it was blown off course. The ship eventually landed on the Massachusetts coast, far outside of the jurisdiction of the Virginia colony. The Pilgrims took matters into their own hands and wrote and signed a brief document by which they would be governed. The Mayflower Compact became the first form of European government in the New World. Time and again, those who came to the New World would take matters into their own hands and devise solutions to problems and shortages that they encountered in the wilderness.

The Pilgrims endured a hard winter, but over the next two years they carved

Religious dissenters, eventually known as Pilgrims, head for ships that will carry them to the New World, where they hope to find religious freedom.

After a treacherous journey across the Atlantic, the first Pilgrims land on the Massachusetts coast. Here they would form the Plymouth colony, dividing up the land into individually owned parcels. The ability to privately own land would continue to be a strong principle in American life.

out a little settlement known as Plymouth. Originally the colonists tried to work their land in a communal fashion. By 1623, the colonists began to break up the land into individually owned lots. William Bradford, who later served as governor of the Plymouth colony, described the steps taken:

> At length, after much debate of things the Gov[ernor] . . . gave way that they should set corne every man for his owne perticuler, and in that regard trust to them selves; in all other things to goe on in the generall way as before. And so assigned to every family a parcell of land, according to the pro-

portion of their number for that end. . . . This had very good success; for it made all hands very industrious, so as much more corne was planted then other waise would have bene by any means the Gov[ernor] or any other could use, and saved him a great deall of trouble, and gave farr better contente.[2]

Like the Virginia colony, the Plymouth colony began to prosper under the new system. The lesson of private land ownership key to these colonists' success was not lost on the generations of Europeans who later came to America. In the future, private ownership of land would become one

Why Early Plantations Failed

In 1629, a year before leading a thousand Puritans to the New World, John Winthrop outlined reasons why other plantations, or colonies, had failed to prosper. Winthrop's observations were published in Puritanism: Opposing Viewpoints.

"Objection 4: The ill success of other plantations may tell us what will become of this[colonization effort].

Answer 1. None of the former sustained any great damage but Virginia; which happened through their own sloth and security.

2. The argument is not good, for thus it stands: some plantations have miscarried, therefore we should not make any. It consists in particulars and so concludes nothing. We might as well reason thus: many houses have been burnt by kilns, therefore we should use none; many ships have been cast away, therefore we should content ourselves with our home commodities and not adventure men's lives at sea for those things which we might live without; some men have been undone by being advanced to great places, therefore we should refuse our preferment, etc.

3. The fruit of any public design is not to be discerned by the immediate success; it may appear in time that former plantations were all to good use.

4. There were great and fundamental errors in the former which are like to be avoided in this, for first their main end was carnal and not religious; secondly, they used unfit instruments—a multitude of rude and misgoverned persons, the very scum of the people; thirdly, they did not establish a right form of government."

of the founding principles of American life, and the quest for land would drive people across the continent.

The success of the Pilgrims inspired another religious group known as the Puritans to embark on its own colonization effort. The Puritans believed they could purify the Anglican Church by removing it from the corruption of England. In 1628,

a group of Puritans incorporated as the Massachusetts Bay Company with the intention of establishing a colony in America. In an essay written the following year, John Winthrop, a wealthy Puritan leader, outlined how migrating to America could save the church:

All other churches of Europe are brought to desolation, and our sins, for which the Lord begins already to frown upon us, do threaten us fearfully, and who knows but that God hath provided this place [the New World] to be a refuge for many whom he means to save out of the general calamity. And seeing the church hath no place left to fly into but the wilderness, what better work can there be than to go before and provide tabernacles and food for her, against she come hither.[3]

Although the Puritans viewed migration to America "to be a work for God for the good of His church,"[4] they recognized social and economic as well as spiritual opportunity. England was still experiencing hard times in the wake of a lengthy war with Spain, and many people lived in poverty. In his essay, Winthrop acknowledged the difficulties that many people had in making a living in England:

We are grown to that height of intemperance in all excess of riot, as no man's estate almost will suffice to keep sail with his equals, and he who fails herein must live in scorn and contempt. Hence it comes that arts and trades are carried in that deceitful and unrighteous course, as it is almost impossible for a good and upright man to maintain his charge and live comfortably in any of them.[5]

In 1630, Winthrop led 1,000 Puritans to the New World. Upon their arrival in Massachusetts, they founded the city of Boston, with Winthrop as governor of the colony. Over the next ten years, Boston's population grew to 24,500 as people fled England to escape severe economic conditions or persecution.

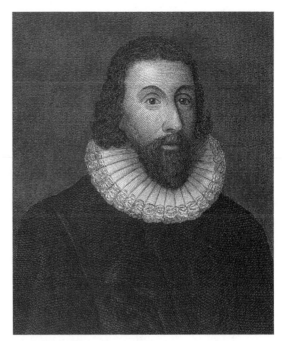

In 1630 John Winthrop led a great migration to Massachusetts, where, as the governor of the Massachusetts Bay Colony, he ruled its inhabitants harshly.

Ironically, Winthrop ruled the colony almost as harshly as the people had been governed in England. Dissenters soon began to leave to establish their own colonies, which became the first settlements of several New England states. In 1635, a group of Puritans led by John Winthrop Jr. established a settlement in what is now Connecticut. The same year, Roger Williams led a group of followers south, where they founded Providence, Rhode Island. Other dissenters from the Massachusetts Bay Colony established the first New Hampshire towns, beginning in 1638 when the Reverend John Wheelwright and a group of followers established Exeter. In this manner, settlements were planted along the coast and up the rivers of New England.

Most of the early New England settlers made their living as farmers, hacking little plots of land out of the forest. The lifestyle of the New England farmer is described by Billington in *Westward Expansion:*

Few New England farmers grew wealthy, but they lived well. Their homes, clustered about the village green, were sturdy frame dwellings, with outbuildings and barns attached to make chores easier during the long winters. Each morning they left their houses to labor in their fields, using crude wooden hoes and mattocks [ax-like tools] fashioned by their own hands, or a clumsy plow pulled by four oxen. Each night they returned, to sit before the broad stone fireplace on fall or winter evenings and build the many necessities that their slender resources did not allow them to buy from England. Everything from plows to furniture was constructed at home; a task in which the wives joined with

A God-Given Right to America

A year before migrating to America in 1630, John Winthrop argued that the Puritans had a God-given right to settle in America on land already occupied by natives. Winthrop's argument was published in Volume 8 of the Proceedings of the Massachusetts Historical Society, *and is reprinted in* Puritanism: Opposing Viewpoints.

"That which lies common and hath never been replenished or subdued is free to any that will possess and improve it, for God hath given to the sons of men a double right to the earth: there is a natural right and a civil right. The first right was natural when men held the earth in common, every man sowing and feeding where he pleased, and then as men and the cattle increased they appropriated certain parcels of ground by enclosing, and peculiar manurance [cultivation], and this in time gave them a civil right. . . . And for the natives in New England, they enclose no land, neither have any settled habitation, nor any tame cattle to improve the land by, and so have no other but a natural right to those countries. So if we leave them sufficient for their use, we may lawfully take the rest, there being more than enough for them and us. Secondly, we shall come in with the good leave of the Natives, who find benefit already by our neighborhood and learn of us to improve part to more use than before they could do the whole. And by this means we come in by valuable purchase, for they have of us that which will yield them more benefit than all the land which we have from them."

Many Native American tribes populated the New World before the arrival of the colonists. Puritans' firm belief that they had a God-given right to Native American lands put the colonists at odds with the native population, whose concept of land use vastly differed from that of the colonists.

their spinning wheels, candle moulds, and churns.[6]

The life of these early farmers was indeed dull in comparison to the lifestyles of the French fur traders or the Spanish conquistadors. But unlike the nomadic French and Spanish, farmers made permanent homes on the land. Their dedication to claiming the land eventually helped the English claim the continent.

Native Resistance

The Puritans' colonization of New England also put them on a collision course with the Native American nations who already lived there. Puritans came to America with the belief that God had granted them the right to settle in the New World. They believed that the natives had failed to make efficient use of the land, and saw

King Philip's War

John Easton, a Puritan colonist, described the outbreak of King Philip's War in 1675 in his narrative "A Relacion of the Indyan Warre." A version of Easton's narrative appears in Original Narratives of Early American History, *published in 1908. Easton's spelling and punctuation have been updated for this book.*

"Plymouth soldiers came to have their headquarters within 10 miles of Philip. Then most of the English thereabouts left their houses and we had a letter from the Plymouth governor to desire our help with some boats if they had such occasion and for us to look to our selves. . . . From the general at the quarters we had a letter that day saying that they intended to come upon the Indians and desired some of our boats to attend, so we took it to be of necessity for our Islanders one half one day and the night to attend and the other half the next, so by turns for our own safety. In this time some Indians fell a pilfering some houses that the English had left, and an old man and a lad going to one of those houses did see 3 Indians run out thereof. The old man bid the young man shoot, so he did and an Indian fell down, but got away again. It is reported that then some Indians came to the garrison [and] asked why they shot the Indian. They asked whether he was dead. The Indians said yea. An English[man] said it was no matter. The men endeavored to inform them it was but an idle lad's words, but the Indians in haste went away and did not harken to them. The next day the lad that shot the Indian and his father and [five] English more were killed so the war begun with Philip."

no reason why they should not take over land that was not being used.

In truth, the natives were using the land. Natives lived a nomadic existence, following the herds of animals they depended upon for food. They returned to semipermanent settlements periodically, depending on the season, but most did not live year-round at the same location. The European concept of land ownership was alien to Native Americans, who believed the land belonged at once to no one and everyone.

When the first Europeans visited the Atlantic coast, Native Americans had for the most part received them warmly. But as Europeans established permanent settlements and appropriated more and more land, the natives began to view the settlers as invaders.

The clash of cultures and interests led to armed conflict within a few years of the

Puritans' arrival. In 1637, war between Pequots and Puritans broke out in Connecticut when Pequots, fearful that they were being squeezed from their hunting grounds by Puritan settlements on either side of them, killed a Boston trader. On May 1, 1637, the colony formally declared war. In a carefully planned military campaign, Puritans overpowered and nearly exterminated the Pequot nation.

Almost forty years later, in 1675, most of New England erupted in warfare as several Native American nations led by a Wampanoag Indian known as King Philip fought the Puritans for control of their rapidly shrinking hunting grounds. King Philip's War was costly for both sides. Native American casualties are unknown, but an estimated five hundred Puritan settlers died. Forty Puritan towns were destroyed or damaged. In August of 1676 King Philip was killed and the war ended with the Puritans in firm control of New England.

The Pequot War and King Philip's War forecast a grim future for Native Americans. Over the next three centuries, frontiersmen and Native Americans would meet in countless clashes across the expanse of the continent, almost always with the identical outcome.

By the end of the 1600s, English settlements had spread along much of Amer-

After fighting for control of hunting grounds, Native American leader King Philip lies dead at the hands of the Puritans.

ica's Atlantic coastline. As the coast became more densely populated, land opportunities became scarce. Colonists born and raised in America, along with waves of emigrant Europeans, headed west in search of new opportunities. The long process of conquering and settling the American continent had begun.

2 Creating a People and a Country

Throughout the eighteenth century, American-born colonists joined by an increasing flow of Europeans from many nations pushed west from coastal and tidewater communities to claim land and establish new settlements in the interior wilderness. By the end of the century the opening and settlement of the west had helped create a new nation, the United States of America.

Settling the Back Country

The west was opened in the same stages as the coast was settled. By the 1650s, with prospering coastal settlements in place, explorers had already begun searching out routes that would lead into the interior. The explorers were followed by trappers and traders who set out in the 1670s and established a thriving fur trade with Native Americans. By 1700, land-hungry settlers and land speculators from New England, Virginia, and the Carolinas began making their way inland to the back country, pushing west until they were stopped by the Appalachian Mountains. The first of these settlers were cattle ranchers, who grazed their herds in the valleys and meadows that broke the forests. Farmers soon followed.

Settlers usually adopted the dress of the Native Americans and fur trappers who preceded them—a fur cap, leggings made of buckskin, and a hunting shirt that hung to the knees and was belted at the waist. With their survival dependent solely on their individual abilities, they became extremely versatile, able to adapt to almost any environment. Frontier men and women developed a strong mechanical ingenuity, which helped them work out solutions to many problems with only the most basic materials.

The essential tools of the western settler were the rifle and the ax. With these two tools, a settler could provide almost everything a family needed. The rifle was used to shoot wild game for food and to protect settlers from aggressive natives or other intruders. The ax was used to clear a few acres of forest that became pastures for livestock or small fields for growing crops. Felled trees were hewed into logs to build a cabin for shelter. The cabin's interior furnishings, even dishes, were made of wood fashioned with an ax. Crude plows and hoes to aid in planting crops were likewise built of wood.

In this isolated, sometimes hostile environment, frontier settlers developed characteristics different from those of their coastal neighbors. They preferred

Early western settlers quickly developed the skills they needed to adapt to their sometimes hostile environment.

simplicity over complexity. Isolated from others and left to their own devices, western settlers developed a deep respect for individualism, a suspicion of authority, and a general impatience with the plodding nature of the colonial government.

The English colonists who moved westward from New England, the Carolinas, and Virginia to the frontier were joined by immigrants from other European nations. In the middle 1700s, Scotch-Irish, German, Dutch, and Swedish immigrants landed on the coast and made their way through the settled regions into the interior where good land was available at little or no cost. Each of these groups contributed something new to the growing frontier culture—Swedish immigrants, for example, introduced simple log cabin construction to the frontier landscape.

For the first time, inhabitants of the back-country frontier settlements were completely cut off from direct European influences, and by the mid-1700s, a separate, unique frontier society had evolved, with a more mixed ethnic composition than the nearly all-English coastal settlements.

Frontier farmers were poor and struggling compared to the more prosperous farmers and merchants who lived back east. Frontier settlers regarded eastern residents as having more in common with England than with themselves. They viewed easterners as land grabbers interested primarily in buying up great quantities of land for speculation. Easterners, on their part, mistook the simple ways of set-

Frontiering Techniques

In 1786, Frenchman François Jean, marquis de Chastellux, described the frontiering techniques he observed while traveling in America between 1780 and 1782. His account is included in volume 2 of American History Told by Contemporaries.

"Any man who is able to procure a capital of five or six hundred livres of our money, or about twenty-five pounds sterling, and who has strength and inclination to work, may go into the woods and purchase a portion of one hundred and fifty or two hundred acres of land. . . . There he conducts a cow, some pigs, or a full sow, and two indifferent horses which do not cost him more than four guineas each. To these precautions he adds that of having a provision of flour and cyder. Provided with this first capital, he begins by felling all the smaller trees, and some strong branches of the large ones; these he makes use of as fences to the first field he wishes to clear; he next boldly attacks those immense oaks, or pines, which one would take for the ancient lords of the territory he is usurping. . . . This object compleated, the ground is cleared; the air and the sun begin to operate upon that earth which is wholly formed of rotten vegetables, and teems with the latent principles of production. The grass grows rapidly; there is pasturage for the cattle the very first year; after which they are left to increase, or fresh ones are bought, and they are employed in tilling a piece of ground which yields the enormous increase of twenty or thirty fold. The next year the same course is repeated; when, at the end of two years, the planter has wherewithal to subsist, and even to send some articles to market; at the end of four or five years, he completes the payment of his land, and finds himself a comfortable planter."

tlers for ignorance and an inability to manage complex social structures such as government.

It did not take long for conflicts to develop between eastern settlements and the frontier. One of the harshest conflicts concerned representation in the colonial legislatures that made local laws. Easterners controlled the legislatures, which allowed them to enact legislation that favored their own interests. Although frontier residents often had a low opinion of government, they nevertheless sought equal representation in it. In 1764, for example, residents of five counties in western Pennsylvania wrote a letter to the governor to complain that as English subjects they were therefore entitled to the same representation as eastern counties. Their grievance drew little action from the governor.

For years this struggle continued throughout the colonies without resolution. Frontier residents never won equal representation in colonial legislatures, but frontier values ultimately prevailed. Respect for equality, individualism, pragmatism, and even impatience became universal attitudes and part of the American character.

Eliminating Barriers

In the mid-1700s, three barriers halted further westward expansion. First, a long chain of mountains that stretched north to south across North America formed a geographic barrier. Competing French interests formed a second barrier; and Native American resistance to settlers a third. During the middle of the eighteenth century, the British government and the American colonists worked to penetrate each of these barriers.

The French Barrier

For over a century, English and French traders had maneuvered against each other for control of the lucrative North American fur trade. The competition for the fur trade was part of a larger, more global conflict between the two nations. Beginning in 1689, they waged a number of wars, both in Europe and on the North American

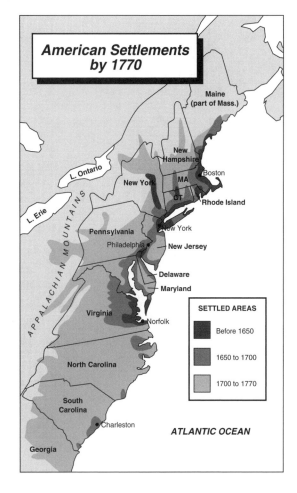

continent, but the outcomes had not resolved the issue of which country would control the North American fur trade.

In 1755, the British launched a new effort to drive the French out of the area west of the mountains. The ensuing Seven Years War was fought in both Europe and North America. The American phase of this war was known as the French and Indian War, the climactic battle of which occurred on September 13, 1759, when British forces under the direction of James Wolfe attacked the French city of Quebec. Both Wolfe and the French commander, the marquis de Montcalm, died in the battle; the British emerged victorious and Quebec surrendered on September 18. A year later, the French city of Montreal also surrendered to the British, and the fighting was over.

The Treaty of Paris, signed in Paris on February 10, 1763, removed the French

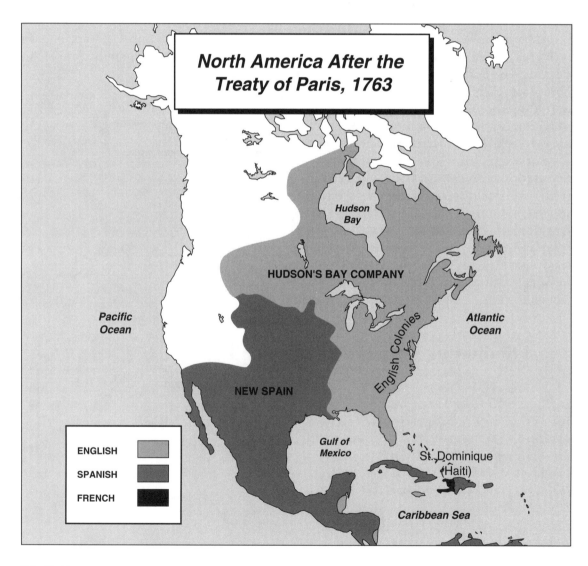

North America After the Treaty of Paris, 1763

Hudson Bay

HUDSON'S BAY COMPANY

Pacific Ocean

Atlantic Ocean

English Colonies

NEW SPAIN

Gulf of Mexico

St. Dominique (Haiti)

Caribbean Sea

ENGLISH

SPANISH

FRENCH

Fatally wounded during the French and Indian War, British general James Wolfe is carried off the battlefield. British victory in the war eliminated the French barrier to westward expansion.

barrier preventing further British expansion to the west. In the treaty, France ceded all but a tiny portion of its holdings in North America to the British. After two centuries, the French empire in North America had disappeared.

The Native American Barrier

Throughout the newly acquired lands, nations of Native Americans greeted the British and their American subjects with suspicion. Some bands had already been cheated by deceitful British fur traders. Others were alarmed at the prospect of having their lands occupied by settlers.

The British were divided over what to do with their new acquisition. Traders wanted the west reserved permanently for natives, which would allow them to continue to develop the fur trade. Land speculators and farmers, on the other hand, wanted the west to be opened for settlement.

Before the British government could develop a policy to satisfy the interests of both groups, Native American resistance broke out across the frontier. In May of 1763, Pontiac, an Ottawa chief, organized a rebellion by Ottawas, Algonquins, some of the Iroquois nations, and tribes along the lower Mississippi River. By October the rebellion faltered, and Pontiac fled into the Illinois wilderness. It took nearly two years of negotiations, however, before peace was completely restored, removing the Native American barrier.

As Pontiac's rebellion faltered, the British government finally issued its land policy. The Proclamation of 1763 tried to address the interests of traders, speculators, and natives. It opened land far to the north and south for settlement. But the proclamation forbade settlement of "any lands beyond the heads or sources of any of the rivers which fall into the Atlantic Ocean from the west or northwest."[7] This irregular boundary line prevented settlers from settling anywhere beyond the eastern slopes of the mountain chain that extended north to south across the continent. The proclamation addressed those who already had settled west of that line:

> And we do further strictly enjoin and require all persons whatever, who have either wilfully or inadvertently seated themselves upon any lands within the countries above described, or upon any other lands which, not having been ceded to or purchased by us, are still reserved to the said Indians as

---

The British–Native American Alliance

In a November 10, 1770, letter to his superior, the earl of Hillsborough, Thomas Gage, commander in chief of the British army in North America, described the relationship between the British and Native American nations in the interior country. Britain's policy toward Native Americans would have slowed settlement of the west by whites. Gage's letter appears in volume 2 of The Annals of America.

"I conceive that to procure all the commerce it will afford, and at as little expense to ourselves as we can, is the only object we should have in view in the interior country for a century to come. . . . Our manufactures are as much desired by the Indians as their peltry is sought for by us; what was originally deemed a superfluity or a luxury to the natives is now become a necessary; they are disused to the bow, and can neither hunt nor make war, without firearms, powder, and lead. The British provinces only can supply them with their necessaries, which they know, and for their own sakes they would protect the trade, which they actually do at present. It would remain with us to prevent the traders being guilty of frauds and impositions. . . .

I know of nothing so liable to bring in a serious quarrel with Indians as an invasion of their property. Let the savages enjoy their deserts in quiet; little bickerings that will unavoidably sometimes happen may soon be accommodated. And I am of opinion, independent of the motives of common justice and humanity, that the principles of interest and policy should induce us rather to protect than molest them. Were they driven from their forests, the peltry trade would decrease."

After leading an unsuccessful rebellion against settlers for two years, Ottawa chief Pontiac ends the fierce fighting by making peace negotiations with the British.

aforesaid, forthwith to remove themselves from such settlements.[8]

The Proclamation of 1763 proved extremely unpopular among Americans who were primarily interested in claiming new land beyond the boundary line. Although the proclamation halted some speculation schemes, it was widely abused by other settlers and speculators who understood that artificial boundaries meant little in the wilderness. Ignoring the boundary and braving attack by natives, they pushed across the mountains to claim land in Kentucky, Tennessee, and the Ohio Valley.

Crossing the Mountain Barrier

The Appalachians still formed a formidable geographic barrier to westward expansion. By the mid-1700s, however, explorers had picked their way through the mountains and back. One of the first white men to cross the mountains into the wilderness and attempt to establish a settlement was a frontiersman named Daniel Boone. In 1769, Boone began an extended hunting trip from North Carolina into Kentucky, not returning home until June 1771. Convinced that his fortunes lay in Kentucky, Boone moved there in 1773 with a small party that included his own family. The venture failed, however, when Boone's eldest son and another settler were killed by Native Americans.

In 1775, Boone tried again. With a party of thirty men he cut a road through the mountains into Kentucky and established a settlement called Boonesborough. The road he created became known as the Wilderness Road, and served as the major highway into Kentucky for many years.

Boone's subsequent experiences were of a variety typical of many frontiersmen who shattered the mountain barrier. In 1778, he was captured by members of the Shawnee nation, but escaped after several months. In later years he became a member of the Kentucky legislature and

Creating a Frontier Legend

With its spectacular account of his capture and escape from the Shawnees, The Life and Adventures of Colonel Daniel Boon, The First White Settler of the State of Kentucky *made Boone a hero and fueled interest in Kentucky and the American frontier. The account was actually written and published in 1782 by land speculator John Filson.*

"On the 10 of April, [the Shawnee] brought me towards Old Chelicothe, where we arrived on the 25th day of the same month. This was a long and fatiguing march, through an exceeding fertile country, remarkable for fine springs and streams of water. At Chelicothe, I spent my time as comfortable as I could expect; was adopted, according to their custom, into a family, where I became a son, and had a great share in the affection of my new parents, brothers, sisters, and friends. . . . I often went a hunting with them, and frequently gained their applause for my activity at our shooting matches. . . . The Shawanese king took great notice of me, and treated me with profound respect, and entire friendship, often entrusting me to hunt at my liberty. I frequently returned with the spoils of the woods, and as often presented some of what I had taken to him, expressive of duty to my sovereign. My food and lodging was in common with them, not so good indeed as I could desire; but necessity made everything acceptable.

I now began to meditate an escape, but carefully avoided giving suspicion.

Until the 1st day of June I continued at Old Chelicothe, and then was taken to the salt springs on Sciota, and kept there ten days making salt. . . .

On my return to Chelicothe, four hundred and fifty of the choicest Indian warriors were ready to march against Boonsborough, painted and armed in a fearful manner. This alarmed me, and I determined to escape.

On the 16 of June, before sunrise, I went off secretly, and reaching Boonsborough on the 20th, a journey of one hundred and sixty miles, during which I had only one meal."

Daniel Boone, hero of the American frontier.

worked as a horse trader and tavern keeper. As a land speculator, he accumulated, then lost, a fortune.

Boone might have slipped into obscurity had it not been for a schoolteacher and Kentucky land speculator named John Filson. In 1782, Filson wrote and published *The Discovery, Settlement and present State of Kentucke*, a promotional work conceived to draw easterners across the Appalachians into Kentucky. One error-filled chapter, titled in part "The Life and Adventures of Colonel Daniel Boon," sensationalized the major events of Boone's life and became so popular that it was published separately in America and England. The tale spurred interest in the frontier and also turned Boone into America's first frontier hero, an embodiment of the values and adventurism of the time. Boone became the prototype for all frontier heroes whose deeds and misdeeds in the winning of the west would be celebrated by future generations of Americans.

The Frontier and American Independence

Settlements like those founded by Daniel Boone sprang up in the west and put American attitudes toward the frontier in direct conflict with the British government's frontier policy. To Americans, the frontier beyond the mountains offered almost unlimited opportunity, and traders, speculators, and settlers wanted unlimited access to it. British officials viewed both colonists and Native Americans as a market for goods manufactured in England. Some officials recognized that the frontier's unlimited potential actually threat-

ened Britain's future control of the colonies. They realized that the continued exploitation of the frontier would make the colonies less dependent upon Britain for manufactured goods.

As early as 1770, Thomas Gage, commander in chief of the British army in North America from 1763 to 1775, warned his superiors of the threat hidden amidst all the opportunity. "As to increasing the settlements to respectable provinces, and colonization in general terms in the remote countries, I conceive it altogether inconsistent with sound policy,"[9] Gage wrote in a letter to the earl of Hillsborough on November 10, 1770. Gage realized that

British commander Thomas Gage feared that if the colonists continued developing the frontier, they would no longer be dependent on the British for manufactured goods.

A Call for Equality

In a 1764 letter to the governor of the colony, residents of five western Pennsylvania counties called for an equal voice in colonial legislatures. The letter appears in the seventh edition of Henry Steel Commager's Documents of American History, *published in 1963.*

"We apprehend that as Freemen and English Subjects, we have an indisputable Title to the same Privileges & immunities with His Majesty's other Subjects who reside in the interior Counties of Philadelphia, Chester, and Bucks, and therefore ought not to be excluded from an equal share with them in the very important Privilege of Legislation; nevertheless, contrary to the Proprietor's Charter and the acknowledged principles of common Justice & Equity, our five counties are restrained from electing more than ten Representatives. . . . This we humbly conceive as oppressive, unequal, and unjust, the cause of many of our Grievances, and an infringement of our Natural privileges of Freedom & Equality."

colonists would soon start manufacturing goods of their own. He was also concerned about Britain's ability to rule its American subjects in so remote a region as the frontier. In his letter, he warned Hillsborough:

They are almost out of reach of law and government; neither the endeavors of government, or fear of Indians has kept them properly within bounds; and it is apparently most for the interest of Great Britain to confine the colonists on the side of the back country, and to direct their settlements along the seacoast, where millions of acres are yet uncultivated.[10]

Gage's accurate perceptions and his warning came too late. American and British views on how to manage and settle the frontier were too far apart to be reconciled. Disagreement over the frontier

was one of many issues that ignited a rebellion by American colonists against British rule.

The rebellion began in the east in 1775, when British troops and colonists clashed in Massachusetts, but it soon spread to the frontier. Both the Americans and the British immediately understood that the key to victory on the frontier was winning the loyalty of the different Native American nations. Because their trading goods were superior to those goods produced in the colonies, the British held a distinct advantage over the Americans. Throughout the war, the American colonists were never very successful in winning the loyalty of the native populations. As a result, they often had to fight the combined forces of the British and their native allies.

Although the colonists waged several successful campaigns against the British in the west, they were unable to break their strength. Many factors contributed to the colonists' failure to win control of the frontier, but the settlers themselves deserved much of the blame. Although they would fight to protect their homes, settlers—individualists that they were—often refused to unite and fight in military campaigns that seemed too far away from home to serve their own interests. For this reason, leaders of the colonial armies were seldom able to secure their victories.

The frontier issue loomed large when the two sides entered peace negotiations in 1782. When negotiations began, American strength on the frontier was at its lowest point of the war. However, though American armies had failed to win the frontier on the battlefield, American diplomats successfully secured the frontier at the peace table.

With the independence of the thirteen American colonies almost a given, the location of the new nation's western border became one of the central points to be negotiated. American diplomats wanted the Mississippi River to be the western boundary, and in taking this position they found they had a surprising ally—one of their enemy. The earl of Shelburne, the chief British diplomat, recognized that western expansion by the Americans was inevitable and that Americans would never be satisfied so long as the path to the west was blocked. He agreed to a border that extended American claims far enough west to allow for plenty of room for future expansion.

By September 3, 1783, both American and English representatives had signed the finalized treaty establishing the independence of the thirteen American colonies. The treaty included the names of each of the colonies in the new nation of the United States of America:

> His Britannic Majesty acknowledges the said United States, viz. New Hampshire, Massachusetts Bay, Rhode Island, and Providence Plantations, Connecticut, New York, New Jersey, Pennsylvania, Delaware, Maryland, Virginia, North Carolina, South Carolina, and Georgia, to be free, sovereign and independent States; that he treats with them as such, and for himself, his heirs and successors, relinquishes all claims to the Government, proprietary and territorial rights of the same, and every part thereof.[11]

In minutely detailed language, citing rivers, lakes, mountain ranges, and artificial lines of latitude and longitude, the treaty established the borders of the new nation. The placement of the western boundary line at the Mississippi was in one sense a recognition of the triumph of American attitudes about the frontier over all others during the eighteenth century. In less than a century, settlement had extended far beyond the Atlantic coast. The frontier had helped to form a distinctly American character and posture, whose values and attitudes had prevailed over those of the French and the British, and were challenging those of the Native American nations that still inhabited frontier lands. Frontier attitudes and frontier people had helped in the creation of a new nation. In the coming years, that nation would set its sights on lands that lay even farther west.

Chapter

3 Unifying a Nation

The treaty of 1783 may have established the independence of the United States on paper, but the ability of the new nation to remain united, withstand foreign challenges, and successfully exploit and protect the frontier it had won at the negotiating table was untested. Along with the new lands, the United States inherited problems that Britain had been unable to solve. The United States also had to contend with the continuing presence of the British on U.S. soil. In devising solutions to these and various other frontier problems, the United States was strengthened and eventually emerged as a more unified nation.

A Dispute over Frontier Ownership

The unity of the new nation and the strength of its government was challenged almost immediately by a dispute over ownership of the frontier lands ceded by Britain to the United States in the 1783 treaty. Several of the original thirteen states claimed ownership of parts of these lands under the original charters granted them by England. For example, Virginia claimed ownership of all lands north and

west of the Ohio River, stretching nearly to Canada, because its 1609 charter gave the colony land "lying from the Sea Coast of the Precinct aforesaid up into the Land, throughout from Sea to Sea, West, and Northwest."[12] In similar fashion, other states located along the Atlantic laid simultaneous claims to the frontier.

These claims touched off a conflict with the five states that had no claims beyond their own borders—Rhode Island, New Jersey, Pennsylvania, Delaware, and Maryland—who argued that the frontier territory was the property of the nation, and the claims of individual states should be ceded or transferred to the federal government. Maryland refused to ratify the Articles of Confederation, the document that governed the United States before the U.S. Constitution was drafted, unless the states holding claims in the frontier ceded their lands to the federal government.

One by one the claimant states bowed to government pressure. In December 1783, Virginia, which had the largest claim, transferred "for the benefit of the said States, all right, title, and claim, as well of soil as jurisdiction, which this commonwealth hath to the territory or tract of country within the limits of the Virginia charter, situate, lying, and being to the northwest of the river Ohio."[13] By 1786, all but a few tiny parcels of land still claimed by Virginia and Connecticut had been ceded to the federal government.

The resolution of this issue was significant in that the interests of the nation as a whole had taken precedence over those of individual states, helping to establish the federal government's authority. The way was now paved for various frontier issues to be addressed by a single national policy, rather than through inconsistent policies adopted by individual states.

Selling and Governing the Frontier

Once the federal government assumed control of the frontier, it had to decide how to sell frontier land to the public and how frontier residents would be governed. Legislation aimed at solving these two problems, though temporary, provided important building blocks for the nation's future policies.

The issue of transferring land was a difficult one. Private ownership of land had already become a cornerstone of American society, but no orderly method of surveying and selling vast quantities of land to settlers and speculators existed. Disputes over land ownership were common. Before the frontier could be settled a workable national policy was necessary.

Congress established such a policy by passing the Ordinance of 1785, providing for the appointment of a surveyor from each state who would

> divide the said territory into townships of six miles square, by lines running due north and south, and others cross-ing these at right angles, as near as may be, unless where the boundaries of the late Indian purchases may render the same impracticable. . . .
>
> The plats [plots] of the townships respectively shall be marked by subdivisions into lots of one mile square, or 640 acres, in the same direction as the external lines, and numbered from 1 to 36.[14]

The ordinance also stated that lots would be sold to the public for a minimum price of $1 per acre.

The Ordinance of 1785 was one of the most important legislative measures in American history. It established both a method for surveying public lands and a procedure for their sale to private owners that remained in use for more than seventy-five years. Today, much of the American landscape bears the distinct physical stamp of the Ordinance of 1785. In many states, roads built on the boundaries of the "lots of one mile square" have imposed a gigantic checkerboard pattern on the topography.

The federal government also had to determine how citizens of the frontier would be governed. The most eager settlers headed west to claim new land in the wilderness without government protection. But others hesitated, fearful that no laws would be in place to resolve disputes that arose. They also wondered if they would have the same rights and privileges on the frontier that they enjoyed in their respective states. Government officials quickly recognized that the absence of frontier government was a barrier to westward movement.

In 1787, Congress passed the Northwest Ordinance, creating a temporary

Making States

Passed by Congress on July 13, 1787, the Northwest Ordinance outlined how frontier lands in the public domain could organize as a territory and eventually become a state. This ordinance helped create many of America's fifty states. This excerpt is taken from the seventh edition of Documents of American History.

"Be it ordained by the United States in Congress assembled, That the said territory, for the purposes of temporary government, be one district, subject, however, to be divided into two districts, as future circumstances may, in the opinion of Congress, make it expedient. . . .

Be it ordained by the authority aforesaid, that there shall be appointed from time to time by Congress, a governor, whose commission shall continue in force for the term of three years, unless sooner revoked by Congress. . . . There shall be appointed from time to time by Congress, a secretary, whose commission shall continue in force for four years unless sooner revoked. . . .

There shall also be appointed a court to consist of three judges, any two of whom to form a court, who shall have a common law jurisdiction. . . .

So soon as there shall be five thousand free male inhabitants of full age in the district, upon giving proof thereof to the governor, they shall receive authority, with time and place, to elect representatives from their counties or townships to represent them in the general assembly. . . .

And, whenever any of the said States shall have sixty thousand free inhabitants therein, such State shall be admitted, by its delegates, into the Congress of the United States, on an equal footing with the original States in all respects whatever, and shall be at liberty to form a permanent constitution and State Government."

governmental district called the Territory North West of the Ohio or, commonly, the Northwest Territory. The ordinance described the ways self-government was to be established in unincorporated territories. It also included a provision for the admission of new states into the Union: When a territory's population reached sixty thousand (defined as "free inhabitants"), it could frame its own constitution and apply for admission to the Union. Once admitted, the new state would have the same status, rights, and privileges as the original thirteen states.

In 1791, Vermont became the first state admitted to the Union after independence. A year later, Kentucky followed, joined by Tennessee in 1796. The first state carved out of the Northwest Territory was Ohio, which was admitted to the Union in 1803.

Although created specifically to address the needs of frontier residents in the Northwest Territory, the 1787 ordinance became one of the great building blocks of American history. Succeeding generations would use the procedures outlined in the ordinance to organize territories and create most of the nation's states.

The Native American Issue

One of the most difficult problems the new nation faced was dealing with the Native American nations who inhabited the frontier. The 1783 treaty between England and the United States was meaningless to the Native Americans, who had hunted the forests and fished the region's lakes and rivers for centuries.

The natives were naturally reluctant to give up their ancestral lands, setting the

A 1791 illustration depicts members of the Creek nation. The Native Americans who already inhabited frontier lands stood ready to resist the advancing settlers.

stage for a bitter conflict with advancing settlers. The already difficult situation was compounded by the British, who wanted to keep control of the fur trade in the Great Lakes area. To keep the Americans on the defensive, they encouraged Native Americans to rebel against the American government.

The U.S. government first attempted to negotiate a series of treaties with various Native American nations. Treaties negotiated from 1784 to 1786 opened the Northwest Territory to Americans for settlement. But the treaties failed at least

General Wayne leads the United States to a decisive victory over the Native Americans at the Battle of Fallen Timbers.

partly because the British continued to undermine them by encouraging natives to revolt against the Americans.

Fighting between Kentucky frontier residents and Native Americans broke out in 1788, and for the next several years the two sides struggled for control of the Ohio Valley. Then in 1791, an American campaign led by Arthur St. Clair ended in a stunning defeat: St. Clair's forces suffered 630 killed and 283 wounded. The victory gave the Native Americans temporary control of the region.

Two years later, the United States began a new campaign to control the Ohio Valley. The deciding confrontation occurred in August 1794 near Ft. Miami, Ohio. Commanded by Gen. Anthony Wayne, the victorious American forces outnumbered the natives two to one. Called the Battle of the Fallen Timbers, Wayne's victory temporarily resolved the struggle for control of the Ohio Valley in favor of the United States. Knowing that siding with the Native Americans against General Wayne could lead to war with the United States, British troops abandoned their native allies. Without aid from the British, the Native Americans were unable to defeat the Americans. The defeated Indians were forced to sign a treaty dictated by victorious General Wayne. When native leaders signed the treaty early in 1795, they ceded most of the Ohio Valley to the United States.

The United States negotiated an additional treaty with the British. Jay's Treaty, signed November 14, 1794, by the United States and Britain, addressed issues that had festered between the two nations since their 1783 treaty. The new treaty gave British fur traders the right to trap in the United States and return their furs to

Canada untaxed. In return, the British agreed to vacate trading posts in U.S. territory that they had illegally held on to after 1783. Despite this concession by the British, the treaty remained unpopular among Americans living on the frontier because they deeply resented the continued presence of British traders on U.S. soil.

Trouble in the Southwest

The two treaties restored an uneasy peace to the Ohio Valley and reopened it for settlement, but the struggling American government faced another foreign challenge in its southwest region. Spain controlled the Florida peninsula and the coast of the Gulf of Mexico, including the mouth of the Mississippi River. Spain's control of access to the Mississippi was a critical obstacle to the development of the frontier. Goods produced in the northwest were floated down the Ohio River until it joined the Mississippi, then down the Mississippi to New Orleans for transfer to oceangoing vessels bound for the east or transatlantic ports. By charging tariffs to pass through New Orleans, Spain influenced the profits of all pioneer farmers and business owners who relied upon the Mississippi.

Fortunately for the American settlers, the Spanish faced political crises in Europe and were willing to negotiate. On October 27, 1795, the two nations signed the Treaty of San Lorenzo, which gave the Americans expanded rights to the port of New Orleans. The treaty also transferred lands in what is now Mississippi and Alabama to the United States.

But to Americans on the frontier, the treaty did not go far enough. They wanted all of Spanish Florida and permanent U.S. control of New Orleans. Before the United States could press the issue, Spain made an unexpected move. On October 1, 1800, Spain signed over to France the entire colony of Louisiana, which stretched northwest from New Orleans toward the Rocky Mountains, all the way to the present-day Canadian border.

The acquisition of New Orleans by France again placed the United States in a vulnerable position regarding its shipping. In an April 18, 1802, letter to Robert R. Livingston, the American minister to France, President Thomas Jefferson outlined the importance of New Orleans to the United States:

To gain access to the primary port to the frontier, Thomas Jefferson (pictured) instructed James Monroe to buy New Orleans from France.

There is on the globe one single spot, the possessor of which is our natural and habitual enemy. It is New Orleans, through which the produce of three-eighths of our territory must pass to market, and from its fertility it will ere long yield more than half of our whole produce, and contain more than half of our inhabitants. France, placing herself in that door, assumes to us the attitude of defiance. . . . These circumstances render it impossible that France and the United States can continue long friends, when they meet in so irritable a position.[15]

The Louisiana Purchase

To eliminate the French threat to American shipping, in 1803 President Jefferson sent James Monroe to Paris to buy New Orleans. The French negotiator stunned Monroe by offering to sell not just New Orleans but the entire colony of Louisiana to the United States. The Louisiana Purchase was completed on April 30, 1803. For payments of $15,000,000 the United States received New Orleans and a total of 828,000 square miles of territory. The purchase gave the United States permanent possession of New Orleans and nearly doubled the size of the nation, extending its western border nearly to the Rocky Mountains.

Besides wresting New Orleans from foreign control, the acquisition of Louisiana stimulated further interest in the frontier. President Jefferson promptly sponsored several parties charged with mapping and exploring Louisiana and the far west. The most famous of these explorers was the team of Meriwether Lewis and

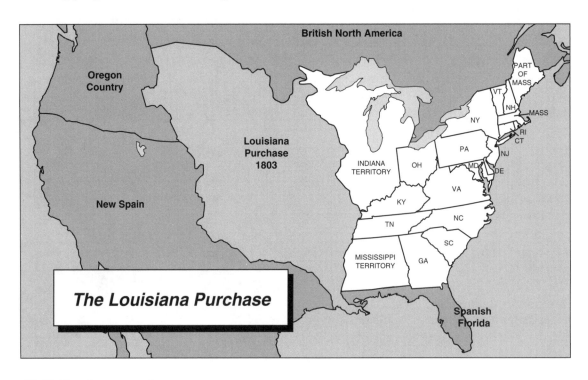

The Louisiana Purchase

The Louisiana Purchase

On April 30, 1803, the following words transferred ownership of the colony of Louisiana from France to the United States. The acquisition of Louisiana doubled the size of the United States, opening a vast frontier to American explorers, traders, and farmers. The document is reprinted in Documents of American History.

"Article I . . . The First Consul of the French Republic desiring to give to the United States a strong proof of his friendship, doth hereby cede to the said United States, in the name of the French Republic, forever and in full sovereignty, the said territory [of Louisiana] with all its rights and appurtenances, as fully and in the same manner as they have been acquired by the French Republic, in virtue of the above mentioned treaty concluded with his Catholic Majesty [of Spain].

Article II. In the cession made by the preceding article are included the adjacent islands belonging to Louisiana, all public lots and squares, vacant lands, and all public holdings, fortifications, barracks, and other edifices which are not private property.—the Archives, papers, and documents, relative to the domain and sovereignty of Louisiana, and its dependencies, will be left in the possession of the Commissaries of the United States, and copies will be afterwards given in due form to the Magistrates and Municipal offices, of such of the said papers and documents as may be necessary to them.

Article III. The inhabitants of the ceded territory shall be incorporated in the Union of the United States, and admitted as soon as possible, according to the principles of the Federal Constitution, to the enjoyment of all the rights, advantages and immunities of citizens of the United States; and in the mean time they shall be maintained and protected in the free enjoyment of their liberty, property, and the Religion which they profess."

William Clark. Their party spent the winter of 1803 near St. Louis, and in April 1804 began their journey up the Missouri River to its source in Montana. From there they journeyed west across the mountains, finally reaching the Pacific Ocean in November 1805.

The expedition's published journals and accounts of other explorers spurred further exploration and settlement of the frontier. Trappers headed west to explore the distant mountains and forests described by Lewis and Clark. A steady stream of settlers continued to journey west in search of new opportunities on the frontier. Those who attempted to settle in the northwest soon encountered two familiar barriers, however—Native American nations and their British allies. These familiar barriers represented yet another challenge to the unity and authority of the United States.

Motives for War

Since the Revolution, Americans had resented British traders and trappers who were allowed to operate in American territory by treaties negotiated in Washington. Their hostility toward the British increased in the years following 1808, when low prices and high shipping costs from the frontier to New Orleans touched off a depression in the Ohio River Valley. Although the long distance between the frontier and its primary port was the main cause of the depression, Americans on the frontier blamed the economic hard times on a naval blockade set up by the British in 1807 to prevent American ships from trading with France, then a British enemy.

In addition to economic hard times and competition from British traders, settlers blamed renewed resistance from Native Americans on the British. Between 1800 and 1810, the United States had secured 110 million acres of Native American land through treaties, threats, and bribery. The natives, however, remained aggrieved by unfair treatment by the U.S. government. In the spring of 1810, they retaliated under the leadership of a Shawnee chief named Tecumseh and his brother, known as the Prophet. By the spring of 1812, warfare between natives and settlers had spread throughout the northwest. Many settlers fled the frontier for the safety of more settled regions in Ohio and Kentucky. Frontier residents blamed the rebellion on the British, who remained allied with many of the Native American nations.

Frontier settlers wanted war with the British. An American victory would rid the region of the British presence once and

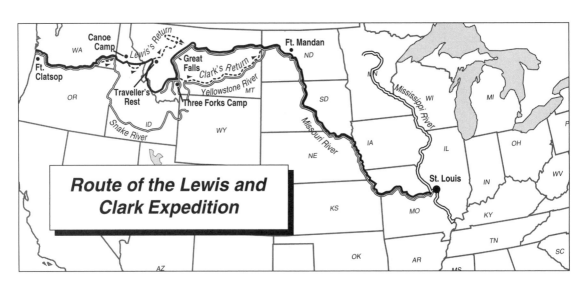

Route of the Lewis and Clark Expedition

for all, break the Native American revolt, and, they believed, reestablish economic prosperity.

Eastern leaders also wanted war, but for different reasons. The British blockade was strangling the eastern economy. Easterners wanted to force Britain to respect the right of American ships to trade freely with other nations.

The United States had negotiated Jay's Treaty to avoid war with the British. Now the U.S. government decided to go to war instead of negotiate. On June 1, 1812, U.S. president James Madison brought the interests of the frontier and the east together in a war message he delivered to the U.S. Congress. Madison declared that the conduct of Britain "presents a series of acts hostile to the United States as an independent and neutral nation."[16] He blamed the hostility between frontier people and Native Americans in the west directly on the British:

> In reviewing the conduct of Great Britain toward the United States our attention is necessarily drawn to the warfare just renewed by the savages on one of our extensive frontiers—a warfare which is known to spare neither age nor sex and to be distinguished by features peculiarly shocking to humanity. It is difficult to account for the activity and combinations which have for some time been developing themselves among tribes in constant intercourse with British traders and garrisons without connecting their hostility with that influence.[17]

Seventeen days after Madison delivered his message, Congress declared that a state of war existed between the United States and Britain.

Shawnee chief Tecumseh sought to unite Native American tribes against encroachment of their ancestral homelands.

The War of 1812

America's strategy in fighting the British was to invade and conquer Canada. With Canada held hostage, the United States hoped to force Britain to respect American independence, and withdraw from American soil for good. In the long run, this strategy failed. In four separate attempts

American forces were unable to defeat the British and capture Canada.

The British also hoped to achieve victory by invasion. British troops successfully invaded the American capital of Washington, D.C., burned the White House, and forced President Madison to flee the city. With the momentum on their side, the British made plans to invade both New York and New Orleans. But the British invasion of New York was stopped at Lake Champlain in the summer of 1814.

This victory marked a turning point in the war. Having achieved few of its military goals, the United States was techni-cally losing the war. Rather than continue fighting, the Americans were willing to negotiate. Faced with the threat of impending war in Europe and unwilling to embark on expensive campaigns to defeat the Americans, the British were also willing to sue for peace.

The two nations entered negotiations in August of 1814. At the negotiating table, American diplomats were able to gain some of the objectives not won on the battlefields. The needs of the frontier, rather than the east, dominated the U.S. strategy in the negotiations. American negotiators agreed to abandon the goal of

Settlers put down a rebellion by Native Americans, killing leader Tecumseh at the Battle of the Thames.

British recognition of America's right to free trade with other nations, provided the British gave up the rights of Canadian traders in the United States. The British readily agreed. The two nations also agreed to return to their original boundaries before the war broke out. The final treaty was signed on December 24, 1814.

Ironically, a final battle in the War of 1812 was fought in early 1815, nearly two

The Illinois Country

On March 25, 1797, Moses Austin, a miner by trade, recorded these observations about the Ohio and Mississippi River Valleys. Native Americans and Americans of European descent battled for this "beautiful and fertile" land in the years following the American Revolution. Austin's observations appear in volume 4 of The Annals of America.

"The Illinois country is perhaps one of the most beautiful and fertile in America and has the peculiar advantage of being interspersed with large plains or prairies and woodlands, where a crop can be made the first year without the trouble and expense of felling the timber, which in every other part of America exhausts the strength and purse of a new settler. The Mississippi affords an easy and certain conveyance for his produce, at all seasons of the year, to New Orleans, which place or some other on the lower parts of the river bids fair to be one of the greatest marts in the world. Nature has undoubtedly intended this country to be not only the most agreeable and pleasing in the world but the richest also. Not that I suppose there are many, if any silver mines or gold dust. Nor do I consider either of them sufficient to make a country rich.

But the Mississippi has what is better—she has a rich landed country. She has the richest lead mines in the world, not only on the Maramag and its waters but also on the banks of the Mississippi, about 700 miles up from St. Louis at a place called Prairie du Chien, or Dog Prairie, at which place, or near it, is also a copper mine of malleable copper, the veins of which are more extensive than any of the kind heretofore found. She has salt springs on each side of the river and also iron ore in great quantities. These minerals are more useful in a country than gold or silver. A country thus rich by nature cannot be otherwise than wealthy with a moderate share of industry."

Andrew Jackson's impressive victory over the British at the Battle of New Orleans made him a hero in the west.

weeks after the peace treaty had been signed. Before news of the war's end reached America from Europe, the British invaded New Orleans. On January 8, 1815, Andrew Jackson, an American officer, led American forces to a stunning victory over the British, killing more than two thousand British troops while suffering only six casualties. Although the Battle of New Orleans had no effect on the outcome of the war, Jackson's victory catapulted him to national fame, making him a hero in the west.

The War of 1812 marked the end of an era in American history. In the years immediately following the Revolution, the United States was untested, united in name only. In solving a number of problems, the U.S. government slowly proved that it could develop successful domestic policies and meet foreign challenges. Frontier settlers and eastern residents had united to fight a common enemy. Independence had been firmly established and the United States faced the future as a more unified nation.

4 Taming the Frontier

With the War of 1812 behind them, Americans once again turned toward the frontier. U.S. possessions extended from the Atlantic Ocean almost to the Rocky Mountains, but most of this vast territory was wilderness. Only a small number of adventuresome trappers and traders had crossed the Mississippi River and journeyed to the far west. East of the Mississippi River, settlement was primarily concentrated in the original thirteen states and in the states created in the Ohio River Valley. Even within these states, frontier conditions persisted, and Native Americans still inhabited their most unsettled regions. For the next twenty-five years, an

A nineteenth-century illustration depicts a settler's homestead in the far west. Before the War of 1812, only a small number of pioneers made the journey to the far west, but within the next twenty-five years scores of settlers crossed the Mississippi River to stake their claims.

ever-increasing tide of American and foreign settlers tamed the frontier east of the Mississippi, and even crossed the great river itself to carve out new settlements.

Taming the Northwest

The removal of the British barrier generated new interest in the frontier known as the Northwest between the Ohio River and the Great Lakes. Like generations of frontier settlers before them, Americans and foreigners alike viewed the Northwest as an opportunity for advancement. Timothy Flint, who traveled the Northwest frontier

Settlers lay fences around their newly claimed land in the Northwest.

between 1815 and 1825 and later published an account of his experiences, observed that the goal of a settler is "to be a freeholder, to have plenty of rich land, and to be able to settle his children about him. This is a most virtuous motive. . . . I fully believe that nine in ten of the emigrants have come here with no other motive."[18]

But one barrier still stood between settlers and "plenty of rich land." Although the British were gone, Native Americans still held claims to their ancestral lands. The eager settlers held no more enlightened views than had their forebears: The natives were savages, they believed, who made no apparent use of the land, and therefore had little real claim to it. Native Americans represented little more than an obstacle to be overcome.

Settlers and land speculators aggressively pressured the U.S. government to open the Northwest for settlement. Between 1817 and 1821, U.S. government agents negotiated treaties with several Native American nations. Knowing that they were no match against the superior number and arms of their opponents, the Native Americans had little choice but to surrender their territories to the U.S. government in exchange for annuities and gifts. In return, they were restricted to life on reservations, or allowed to move to the wilderness beyond the Mississippi. By the end of 1821, Native Americans had ceded most of the Northwest to the federal government.

The newly opened territory attracted a steady stream of settlers from all parts of the United States. They were joined by immigrants from England, Germany, France, Ireland, and Norway, who left their old lives behind in search of prosperity on the frontier.

Crowds of Inhabitants

Circuit court judge James Hall described the wide range of people who journeyed to the Mississippi Valley to try their hand at taming the frontier. Hall's impressions, published in London in 1828 under the title Letters from the West, *are taken from* Annals of America, *volume 5.*

"English, Irish, French, and Germans are constantly emigrating to the new states and territories; and all the Eastern, Southern, and Middle states send them crowds of inhabitants; nor is the needy and unfortunate alone who bury themselves among the shadows of the Western forests.

There was a time, indeed, when the word 'emigration' carried with it many unpleasant sensations; and when we heard of a respectable man hieing to an unknown land, to seek a precarious existence among bears and mosquitoes, we fancied that we saw the hand of a land speculator beckoning him to destruction, and pitied his fate. . . . But that is not the fact now; whatever might have been the case a few years ago, we now find classes of people among the emigrants who would not be easily deluded. Gentlemen of wealth and intelligence, professional men of talents and education, and respectable farmers and artisans have, after dispassionate inquiry, determined to make this country their future abode."

The forest lands were often claimed first, because new arrivals could draw on the experience of northeastern settlers who had already mastered the techniques necessary to tame wooded lands. But as the forest lands were claimed, subsequent arrivals were forced to settle on the open prairies. To cultivate this terrain, frontier people developed a whole new frontiering technique. Lumber was shipped in to be converted into shelter. Settlers learned to dig deep wells for water. New plows were developed to break up the thick prairie sod.

Life on the northwestern frontier was often lonely and difficult. Morris Birbeck, an English immigrant who settled in the territory of Illinois, described the isolated conditions he encountered shortly after his arrival:

These lonely settlers are poorly off: their bread corn must be ground thirty miles off, requiring three days to carry to the mill, and bring back the small horse-load of three bushels. Articles of family manufacture are very scanty, and what they purchase is of the meanest quality and excessively dear: yet they are friendly and willing to share their simple fare with you. It is surprising how comfortable they seem, wanting every thing. To struggle with privations has now become the habit of their lives, most of them having made several successive plunges into the wilderness: and they begin already to talk of selling their "improvements," and getting still farther "back," on finding that emigrants of another description are thickening about them.[19]

Blackhawk's War

As the frontier was pushed farther and farther north and west from the Ohio River, settlers encountered new resistance from Native Americans. The federal government responded by adopting an even harsher Native American policy. Settlers so coveted land that the government abandoned its policy of allowing natives who ceded their land to live on reservations among the settlers. Instead, the government moved toward a policy favoring complete removal of all natives east of the Mississippi. This policy soon led to new conflicts. Perhaps the bloodiest conflict during this era was Blackhawk's War, which took place where the present states of Iowa, Wisconsin, and Illinois come together.

For years after the arrival of settlers, Blackhawk, a sixty-year-old Sauk chief, refused to leave his homeland. In 1831, a force of fifteen hundred militia was organized to march against Blackhawk and his followers. Blackhawk retreated across the Mississippi, where he and his followers spent a miserable winter. During that long

Sauk chief Blackhawk and his followers suffered a devastating loss at the hands of the settlers when Native Americans tried to resist U.S. attempts to remove them from their homelands.

winter, Blackhawk experienced a vision of peace and prosperity in his homeland. He decided to return and explain to the Americans that he and his followers only wanted to live quietly on their ancestral lands.

In April 1832, Blackhawk's band of 1,000, including 600 women and children, began the trek back to their homeland. Again a militia was raised by settlers, and in May, Blackhawk and his band were attacked as they attempted to surrender. The incident made Blackhawk realize war was inevitable. By the end of July, Blackhawk's band had killed 200 whites, losing an equal number of their own. Before summer's end, Blackhawk's band was trapped between soldiers on the banks of the Mississippi and a gunboat patrolling its waters. After a three-hour battle, only 150 of the original band of 1,000 natives that had crossed the river several months earlier remained alive.

Blackhawk's defeat sealed the fate of Native Americans in the Northwest frontier. The few remaining Native Americans were relocated over the next five years, opening the far reaches of the Northwest for settlement. Americans and immigrants rapidly claimed the land, and by the end of the 1830s, the wilderness in the farthermost reaches of the Northwest frontier was being replaced by farms and towns.

Taming the Southwest

At the same time that settlers were taming the Northwest, other settlers began pushing into the plains east of the Mississippi River and north of the Gulf of Mexico, known as the Southwest. The opening of the frontier there had been slowed by the ready availability of good lands in Georgia and Tennessee. Poor transportation routes and a lack of communication with the settled areas to the east had also hampered settlement.

The invention of a simple mechanical device helped to touch off a clamor for new land throughout the southern part of the country. Although the southern climate was ideal for growing cotton, cotton was not a profitable crop because it was difficult to process. It took all day for one worker to separate one or two pounds of cotton from its seeds. In 1792 Eli Whitney invented a mechanical device that quickly and efficiently separated cotton fibers from their seeds. With improvements, Whitney's cotton gin could separate up to a thousand pounds of cotton fibers per

Backwoodsmen

In his memoir Recollections of the Last Ten Years, *missionary Timothy Flint describes the frontierman, or backwoodsman, he encountered in his work in the Mississippi and Ohio Valleys. His recollections, published in 1826, appear in volume 5 of* Annals of America.

"You find, in truth, that he has vices and barbarisms peculiar to his situation. His manners are rough. He wears, it may be, a long beard. He has a great quantity of bear- or deerskins wrought into his household establishment, his furniture, and dress. He carries a knife or a dirk [long-bladed dagger] in his bosom and when in the woods has a rifle on his back and a pack of dogs at his heels. An Atlantic stranger, transferred directly from one of our cities to his door, would recoil from an encounter with him. But remember that his rifle and his dogs are among his chief means of support and profit. Remember that all his first days here were passed in dread of the savages. Remember that he still encounters them, still meets bears and panthers."

The invention of the cotton gin in 1792 by Eli Whitney turned cotton into a highly profitable crop, causing throngs of planters to move to the Southwest to grow cotton.

day. The success of Whitney's invention soon made cotton the number one crop in the south.

Planters flocked to the broad plains, intending to develop new cotton plantations. Many of them came from the Carolinas and the Georgia coast, where they had worn out their land by planting the same crops year after year.

More Resistance from Native Americans

Like settlement in the Northwest, the advance of planters into the Southwest was met with resistance from the Native American nations that inhabited the region. The planters who settled on these plains viewed Native Americans with the same prejudices as did northern frontiersmen. The elimination of the Native American barrier in the Southwest frontier was greatly aided by the election of Andrew Jackson to the presidency in 1828. As the first American president born on the frontier, Jackson clearly understood frontier issues. He applied the same pragmatism in addressing frontier issues from Washington, D.C., that settlers applied to solving problems on the frontier. Jackson soon made it clear that his intentions were to open native lands for white settlement.

In his first message to Congress on December 8, 1829, Jackson pointed out the hypocrisy of government policy toward Native Americans. "Professing a desire to civilize and settle them, we have at the same time lost no opportunity to purchase their lands and thrust them farther into the wilderness," he told Congress. "Thus, though lavish in its expenditures upon the subject, government has constantly defeated its own policy, and the Indians, in general, receding farther and farther to the west, have retained their savage habits."[20]

Jackson predicted extinction for the Choctaw, the Cherokee, and the Creek nations if this policy continued. To prevent this grim fate, Jackson proposed an alternative:

I suggest for your consideration the propriety of setting apart an ample district west of the Mississippi, and without the limits of any state or territory now formed to be guaranteed to the Indian tribes, as long as they shall occupy it, each tribe having a distinct control over the portion designated for its use. There they may be secured in the enjoyment of governments of their own choice, subject to no other control from the United States than

Whites and Savages Can't Live Together

In 1830, President Andrew Jackson explained to Congress why white settlers could not accept "savages" on lands they coveted, then offered a solution. This text is taken from Francis Newton Thorpe's The Statesmanship of Andrew Jackson as Told in His Writings and Speeches, *published in 1909.*

"What good man would prefer a country covered with forests and ranged by a few thousand savages to our extensive Republic, studded with cities, towns, and prosperous farms, embellished with all the improvements which art can devise or industry execute, occupied by more than 12,000,000 happy people, and filled with all the blessings of liberty, civilization, and religion? . . . The waves of population and civilization are rolling to the westward, and we now propose to acquire the countries occupied by the red men of the South and West by fair exchange, and, at the expense of the United States to send them to a land where their existence may be prolonged and perhaps made perpetual. Doubtless it will be painful to leave the graves of their fathers; but what do they more than our ancestors did or than our children are now doing?"

such as may be necessary to preserve peace on the frontier and between the several tribes.[21]

Congress was more than willing to make Jackson's proposal official. The next year, Congress passed a law formalizing removal as the government's official policy toward dealing with Native Americans living east of the Mississippi.

The Plight of the Cherokee

Not all of the Native American nations living east of the Mississippi had "retained their savage habits" as Jackson claimed. Many had embraced part or all of the culture of the Americans. In the state of

Upon his election, President Andrew Jackson made it evident that he wished to remove the Native Americans from the Southwest and open the land to settlers.

Cherokee Alphabet

D.		R.	T.	δ.	C.	i.

Convinced that the lack of a written language left his tribe at a disadvantage with whites, Sequoya developed an alphabet for use by the Cherokee in 1821.

Georgia, where frontier conditions still existed, the 15,000-member Cherokee nation owned 22,000 cattle, 1,300 slaves, 2,000 spinning wheels, 700 looms, 31 gristmills, 10 sawmills, and 8 cotton gins, and operated 18 schools. The nation had a written language, published its own newspaper, and in 1827 established its own government.

Despite the fact that the Cherokee seemed a model of what the U. S. government wanted Native Americans to be, Georgia residents favored removal of the Cherokee from the state, if for no other reason than to claim their land. When the Georgia legislature passed a resolution ordering the Cherokee to turn over their lands to the state, the Cherokee sued the state of Georgia, claiming it was a foreign nation and not answerable to Georgia state law. The case eventually went all the way to the U.S. Supreme Court, which ruled in favor of the State of Georgia. The Cherokee issue came before the Supreme Court again in a different case, *Worcester vs. Georgia:* This time, the Court ruled that the Cherokee nation was independent of Georgia law, but was answerable instead to the federal government.

After losing their homelands in Georgia to the U.S. government, the Cherokee people were forced to move west. Their thousand-mile trek resulted in the death of one-fourth of their tribal members.

The favorable ruling proved to be a meaningless victory for the Cherokee. Upon hearing the decision, President Jackson is said to have retorted that as Chief Justice John Marshall had issued the ruling, Marshall himself could enforce it.

These court cases only delayed the inevitable. U.S. government agents soon found a small faction of Cherokee people willing to cede the nation's claims in Georgia to the government for $5.6 million. It was this transaction, rather than the Supreme Court decision, that was enforced by the U.S. government. Over the next three years, defeated Cherokee moved west in small, ragged bands to the territory that Jackson had outlined in his first address to Congress. Many died along the way. The last of the Cherokee were driven west by troops in December 1838. A quarter of the band perished on the way.

Throughout the Southwest, other Native American nations were relocated in a similar fashion. With the removal of the native barrier complete, the Southwest frontier filled in rapidly as planters carved out great cotton plantations. These plantations soon became the foundation of both the region's economy and its society.

New States

By 1840, the quest to tame the frontier and exploit its opportunities had resulted in remarkable changes to U.S.-owned territory east of the Mississippi River. The frontier was rapidly disappearing in the Northwest and Southwest, replaced by farms, small villages, and new cities. All of the land east of the Mississippi River had been organized into territories or divided into states.

Under guidelines established by the Northwest Ordinance of 1787, the United States had grown from eighteen states in 1815 to a total of twenty-six states. Seven of the eight new states had been carved from land that had been mostly wilderness just thirty years earlier. In the Northwest, Indiana was admitted to the Union in 1816, followed by Illinois in 1818 and Michigan in 1837. In the Southwest, Mississippi became a state in 1817, followed by Alabama in 1818. Settlement had also jumped across the Mississippi River, where land was highly suitable for growing cotton. Missouri and Arkansas, admitted to the Union in 1821 and 1836, repectively, became the first American states west of the Mississippi.

A significant percentage of the nation's population now lived in frontier states. In 1810, only 103,000 people lived in the area later encompassed by the new states of Indiana, Illinois, Michigan, Alabama, Mississippi, Missouri, and Arkansas—a mere 1.4 percent of the nation's population of 7,239,881. By 1840, the population of the United States had more than doubled, increasing to more than 17,000,000. But a far greater proportion of the nation's total population now lived in the west. According to the 1840 U.S. census, the population of these seven frontier states was 2,823,000, 16.5 percent of the nation's population.

Spreading Democracy

As people moved west across the continent, American democracy also moved west but in an altered form. Those who created frontier government usually

The "Boundless Continent"

In Democracy in America, *published in 1835, Alexis de Tocqueville linked the tradition of democracy in America to the frontier, which he referred to as the "boundless continent."*

"The chief circumstance which has favored the establishment and the maintenance of a democratic republic in the United States, is the nature of the territory which the Americans inhabit. Their ancestors gave them the love of equality and of freedom; but God himself gave them the means of remaining equal and free, by placing them upon a boundless continent. General prosperity is favorable to the stability of all governments, but more particularly of a democratic one, which depends upon the will of the majority, and especially upon the will of that portion of the community which is most exposed to want. When the people rule, they must be rendered happy, or they will overturn the state: and misery stimulates them to those excesses to which ambition rouses kings. The physical causes, independent of the laws, which promote general prosperity, are more numerous in America than they ever have been in any other country in the world, at any other period of history. In the United States, not only is legislation democratic, but Nature herself favors the cause of the people."

French political scientist Alexis de Tocqueville analyzed the role of the frontier in shaping democracy in America.

sought to curtail its power as much as possible. In drafting new charters and constitutions, framers usually used eastern models, lifting clauses that limited government, and rejecting clauses that gave it more power. For example, the Ohio and Illinois constitutions excluded clauses that gave the governor the power to veto laws passed by the legislature, an exclusion that kept the power of making legislation firmly in the hands of legislators. Western governments also tended to impose shorter terms for elected officials. Clauses which required men to own property before they could vote were omitted from western constitutions. Such limitations made western governments more democratic than eastern governments.

But some saw a potential danger in limiting central authority in favor of unrestricted majority rule. Alexis de Tocqueville, a French political scientist, toured America between May 1831 and February 1832, studying the nation and its people. In *Democracy in America*, published three years later, de Tocqueville observed :

> The very essence of democratic government consists in the absolute sovereignty of the majority. . . . The majority [in America] exercise a prodigious actual authority, and a power of opinion which is nearly as great; no obstacles exist which can impede or even retard its progress, so as to make it heed the complaints of those whom it crushes upon its path. This state of things is harmful in itself, and dangerous for the future.[22]

De Tocqueville could no doubt have pointed to the removal of Native Americans from the territory east of the Mississippi River as an example of the "absolute sovereignty of the majority" at work. Most Americans had favored removal of Native Americans to open land for settlement, and nothing had retarded their progress. American settlement was advancing at the cost of a way of life for an entire race of people.

Romanticizing the Frontier

Even as most Americans busied themselves with taming the frontier and spreading democracy, a few recognized that something undefinable but nevertheless important was being lost. In 1823, James Fenimore Cooper published *The Pioneers*, a novel set in upper New York State. In this book Cooper raised important issues about the spoiling of the wilderness and the corrupting influence of the spread of civilization. His hero, Natty Bumppo, witnesses the displacement of the wilderness by civilization. After many adventures, Natty finally rejects the corruption of civilization and returns to the wilderness.

James Fenimore Cooper's novels raised the issue of the corrupting influence of civilization.

Unfortunately, the book's serious issues were overshadowed by its hero. Whether intentionally or not, Cooper romanticized both the frontier and Natty Bumppo, whom he modeled after Daniel Boone. Natty was intelligent, agile, a skilled woodsman, and the master of every situation he encountered. He immediately captured the fancy of Cooper's audience, even as they continued to destroy the wilderness around them. Readers were fascinated with Natty's frontier attire and habits and his love of the wilderness, the same qualities they had rejected in Native Americans.

Exactly how greatly Natty influenced Americans who lived during the 1830s to head west cannot be determined. But Cooper's own success indicates that he had found a character who captured the American imagination. The novel proved so popular that Cooper followed it with *The Last of the Mohicans* (1826) and *The Prairie* (1827). In the latter novel, he killed off Natty Bumppo, but readers refused to let Natty go. By popular demand, Cooper wrote two additional novels about Natty's early life, *The Pathfinder* (1840) and *The Deerslayer* (1841).

This group of Cooper's novels, collectively known as the *Leatherstocking Tales*, helped establish the frontier hero and the taming of the frontier as part of the nation's mythology. Natty Bumppo became one of the cornerstones in American literature and remains a mythic figure in the American imagination even today.

By the time the last of Cooper's novels about Natty Bumppo appeared in print, the land east of the Mississippi was rapidly filling up. Americans and immigrants alike continued to view the west as a land of opportunity. Americans, in fact, had come to believe it was their destiny to control the continent. By the end of the 1840s, Americans had pushed the territorial limits of the United States all the way to the Pacific Ocean.

Chapter

5 Manifest Destiny

Even as the territory east of the Mississippi was being settled, the distant frontiers that extended to the Pacific Ocean beckoned Americans, as the Atlantic frontier had beckoned the Puritans, and Kentucky had beckoned Virginia colonists. The United States owned much of this western territory, but much of it was owned by other countries. In the far southwest, three Mexican provinces—Texas, New Mexico, and California—lay between the United States and the Pacific. In the far northwest, the United States and Britain jointly occupied a large area known as Oregon.

Many Americans believed that it was America's destiny to control all of the North American continent. During the first half of the nineteenth century, this belief, which was eventually given the name "manifest destiny," strongly influenced the attitudes of Americans and the policies of the U.S. government.

The Origins of Manifest Destiny

The origins of manifest destiny in America date back to the first Puritan settlements on the Atlantic frontier. The Puritans came to the New World with the belief that they had a God-given right to settle on land already occupied by Native Americans and worship as they pleased. The notion that they were God's chosen people remained fixed in the minds of Americans as they moved farther and farther west. Americans viewed their success in taming the frontier, their triumph over Native Americans, and the creation of a new nation as proof that they were indeed God's chosen people.

If more proof was needed, scientists in America and Europe were publishing books and articles claiming the superiority of Caucasians, or white people, to other races. In 1830, for example, Charles Caldwell, an American physician, published *Thoughts on the Original Unity of the Human Race.* In this book, Caldwell argued that God had not created a single race, as the Bible taught, but four races of people, Caucasian, Mongolian, Indian, and African. God himself had created Caucasians as a superior race, Caldwell believed. "To the Caucasian race," Caldwell wrote, "is the world indebted for all the great and important discoveries, inventions, and improvements, that have been made in science and the arts."[23]

When Americans of Caucasian origin compared the "primitive" Native American and African cultures they had encountered through the years to their own "civilized" culture, many easily accepted Caldwell's claims that they were the superior race. It became equally easy for many Americans to use their alleged superiority to justify such actions as killing and removing Native Americans from their homeland and the ownership of African slaves.

Economic and political motives were mixed into the spirit of manifest destiny as well. The religious fervor that had brought the Puritans to the Atlantic coast had long since given way to a fervor to exploit the economic opportunity provided by the frontier. Americans perceived the western frontier beyond the Mississippi as a land of unlimited opportunity, and they wanted to claim that opportunity for themselves. Politicians who remembered British interference in America after the Revolution or the insecurity caused by foreign control of the port of New Orleans believed that if the claims of other countries were eliminated from the continent, the interests and safety of the United States would be more secure.

All of these motives and attitudes convinced Americans that the beckoning continent was theirs for the taking, and that it was their destiny to take it. As early as 1818, an unknown American pioneer declared: "Our western boundary will, ultimately, be the Pacific Ocean."[24] Shortly afterwards, in the spirit of manifest destiny, American settlers headed west to the Mexican province of Texas.

Lured by promises of opportunity, a pioneer family makes the long journey from Arkansas to Texas, hoping to take advantage of Texas's vast resources.

A Clash of Cultures

The boundary between the United States and the Mexican province of Texas had been set in a treaty signed by the United States and Spain in 1819, before Mexico won its independence. Many Americans resented the treaty, however, claiming that the United States had wrongly ceded Texas to Spain. Beginning in 1821, scores of Americans ignored the boundary and staked out claims on the east Texas lowlands, where conditions were ideal for growing cotton. Though peaceful, their entry into Texas set the stage for a clash between the American and Mexican cultures.

There were many differences between the two cultures. Most obvious was the difference in skin color. Mexicans had darker skin than Americans, which led many Americans to regard Mexicans as inferior. Mexico had officially become a democracy when it gained independence from Spain. However, the Mexican government often followed the traditions of the Spanish monarchy, which centralized power in the hands of a small elite. American democracy, in theory at least, distributed power in the hands of many people. Mexican society remained divided into distinct social classes, while Americans professed a strong preference for social equality, even if they failed to practice it. Ironically, slavery was permitted in the United States but was opposed in Mexico.

The two cultures also had different religious backgrounds. Mexico was a Catholic nation and its citizens were expected to follow the teachings of the Catholic Church. Largely Protestant America favored religious freedom and the separation of church and government.

Because of these cultural differences, many Americans viewed themselves as superior to the Mexican people. They used their self-proclaimed superiority to justify their encroachment of Mexican territory, just as their ancestors had justified their treatment of Native Americans for nearly two hundred years.

By 1830 eastern Texas was largely occupied by American settlers, although it was a Mexican province and the people who lived there were subject to Mexican law. Fearing it would lose its province to the United States, Mexico took steps to strengthen its control over Texas, increasing its troop strength there and passing legislation prohibiting further settlement in Texas by Americans.

Texas Independence

American settlers in Texas viewed the measures Mexico had taken as limits to their own freedom, and some began to speak out for independence. Late in 1835, one group of Texans defied the Mexican government by forming its own provisional government. The group appointed a commission of three to visit the United States to solicit aid, then adjourned with plans to meet again on March 1, 1836.

Before that meeting took place, war broke out between Texas patriots and Mexican soldiers under the command of General Antonio López de Santa Anna. Santa Anna had established himself as dictator of Mexico, and set out from Mexico City to break the Texas independence movement.

On February 23, 1836, Santa Anna attacked the small Alamo mission near San

Predicting War with Mexico

Alexis de Tocqueville described the conflict between Mexico and the Anglo-Americans (Britain and the United States) for control of the west. His observations, which foreshadowed the annexation of Texas and the Mexican War, appear in Democracy in America.

"To the northwest, nothing is to be met with but a few insignificant Russian settlements; but to the southwest, Mexico presents a barrier to the Anglo-Americans. Thus the Spaniards and the Anglo-Americans are properly speaking, the two races which divide the possession of the New World. The limits of separation between them have been settled by treaty; but although the conditions of that treaty are favorable to the Anglo-Americans, I do not doubt that they will shortly infringe it. Vast provinces, extending beyond the frontiers of the Union towards Mexico, are still destitute of inhabitants; the natives of the United States will people these solitary regions before their rightful occupants. They will take possession of the soil, and establish social institutions, so that, when the legal owner at length arrives, he will find the wilderness under cultivation, and strangers quietly settled in the midst of his inheritance.

The lands of the New World belong to the first occupant; they are the natural reward of the swiftest pioneer. Even the countries which already are peopled will have some difficulty in securing themselves from this invasion. I have already alluded to what is taking place in the province of Texas. The inhabitants of the United States are perpetually migrating to Texas, where they purchase land; and although they conform to the laws of the country, they are gradually founding the empire of their own language and their own manners. The province of Texas is still part of the Mexican dominions, but it will soon contain no Mexicans; the same thing has occurred wherever the Anglo-Americans have come in contact with a people of a different origin."

Antonio. In the ten-day siege that followed, all 187 of the Alamo's defenders were killed, including two famous American frontiersmen, Davy Crockett and Jim Bowie. The battle became a rallying point for Texans. Cries of "Remember the Alamo!" inspired politicians and soldiers alike in the fight for independence.

A nineteenth-century lithograph depicts the 1836 siege of the Alamo (above), where 187 Texan defenders were killed in the struggle for independence from Mexico. Frontiersman Sam Houston (below) was a leader in Texas's quest to become an independent republic.

A delegation of 59 Texans convened on March 1, 1836, and declared Texas's independence from Mexico. Sam Houston, an American who had settled in Texas, was named commander in chief of the army. On April 21, 1836, Houston's army clashed with the Mexican army in east Texas. The victorious Texans killed 630 Mexican soldiers and captured 730, including Santa Anna, leader of the Mexican army. Mexico was unable to mount a counteroffensive, and Texas was free from Mexican rule.

The Annexation of Texas

Texas was now an independent republic, but in both Texas and the United States, the future relationship between the two republics was immediately a hotly debated

Eager to expand the borders of the United States, President James Polk pushed for the annexation of Texas.

he left office early in 1845, U.S. president John Tyler, a strong proponent of U.S. expansion toward the Pacific, mustered enough support to push an annexation bill through Congress.

Tyler's successor, James K. Polk, continued Tyler's efforts to bring Texas into the Union. In his inaugural address on March 4, 1845, Polk addressed the importance of statehood to Texas and the United States. Polk's speech neatly tied together the political and economic motivations of America's expansionist policy. Polk claimed that the expansion of America's borders expanded peace. "Our Union is a confederation of independent States, whose policy is peace with each other and all the world," he told his listeners. "To enlarge its limits is to extend the dominions of peace over additional territories and increasing millions."[25] By joining the United States, Texas would be under "the strong protecting arm" of the United States, which in return, would guarantee the "safety of New Orleans and of our whole southwestern frontier against hostile aggression."[26]

Behind Polk's political justifications lurked strong economic motivations. Statehood was important to Texas, Polk claimed, because "the vast resources of her fertile soil and genial climate would be speedily developed."[27] Polk undoubtedly knew that eager U.S. settlers would quickly move to Texas to help develop her vast resources. Tying his political and economic motivations together, Polk concluded:

> None can fail to see the danger to our safety and future peace if Texas remains an independent state or becomes an ally or dependency of some

political issue. Leaders of both countries favored U.S. annexation, or acquisition, of Texas, but Texans wanted advance assurance of statehood. In America, Texas statehood was connected to the growing slavery issue. Southerners who supported slavery favored annexation and the admission of Texas as a slave state. Northerners who opposed slavery feared that annexation and statehood would extend slavery.

For nearly a decade, these and other issues stalled the annexation of Texas by the United States. Ultimately, however, the spirit of manifest destiny prevailed. Before foreign nation more powerful than herself. Is there one among our citizens who would not prefer perpetual peace with Texas to occasional wars, which so often occur between bordering independent nations? Is there one who would not prefer free intercourse with her to high duties on all our products and manufacturers which enter her ports or cross her frontiers? Is there one who would not prefer an unrestricted communication with her citizens to the frontier obstructions which must occur if she remains out of the Union?[28]

Although the Mexican government no longer had any real control over Texas, it had never recognized Texas independence. In May 1845, Mexico made a final effort to mitigate Texas's loss by offering to recognize its independence provided Texas did not annex itself to a foreign government. The Mexican offer may have prompted publication of an unsigned editorial in the July issue of the *Democratic Review*. Addressing the issue of Texas statehood, the editorial said that if a reason was needed to justify statehood,

> it surely is to be found, found abundantly, in the manner in which other nations have undertaken to intrude themselves into [the statehood issue] between us and the proper parties to the case, in a spirit of hostile interference against us, for the avowed object of thwarting our policy and hampering

Creating the State of Texas

On March 1, 1845, a joint resolution passed by the House and U.S. Senate annexed the republic of Texas to the United States. Texas became a state on December 29, 1845. The resolution is reprinted in Documents of American History.

"*Resolved . . .*, That Congress doth consent that the territory properly included within, and rightfully belonging to the Republic of Texas, may be erected into a new State, to be called the State of Texas, with a republican form of government, to be adopted by the people of said republic, by deputies in convention assembled, with the consent of the existing government, in order that the same may be admitted as one of the States of this Union. . . .

Be it resolved, That a State, to be formed out of the present Republic of Texas . . . shall be admitted into the Union, by virtue of this act, on an equal footing with the existing States, as soon as the terms and conditions of such admission, and the cession of the remaining Texian territory to the United States shall be agreed upon by the Governments of Texas and the United States."

our power, limiting our greatness and checking the fulfilment of our manifest destiny to overspread the continent allotted by Providence for the free development of our yearly multiplying millions.[29]

Scholars later attributed this unsigned editorial to *Democratic Reveiw* editor John L. O'Sullivan. In giving voice to his beliefs, O'Sullivan also gave a name to the expansionist sentiment that was to guide American policy. In the years that followed, Americans spoke of fulfilling their "manifest destiny" to rule the continent.

When it was decided that Texas could enter the Union as a slave state, Texans selected statehood over the Mexican offer of independence. In December, President Polk announced that Texas had submitted its constitution. On December 29, 1845, Texas became the twenty-eighth state to join the Union.

War with Mexico

The United States had avoided war with Mexico over Texas, but America's expansionist doctrine of manifest destiny ultimately resulted in war between the two nations. The issues that led to war between the United States and Mexico were complex, but basically the source of the conflict was simple: The United States was determined to acquire Mexico's northern provinces of California and New Mexico for future settlement and to eliminate any foreign influence between U. S. territory and the Pacific Ocean. Mexico rightly owned these provinces and was equally determined to keep them.

In 1845, Polk set out to acquire New Mexico and California by whatever means necessary. He sent an agent named John Slidell to Mexico City, authorized to buy California and New Mexico outright from Mexico. Slidell was also instructed to resolve a dispute over the boundary line between the state of Texas and Mexico. The United States claimed that the southern boundary of Texas was the Rio Grande. Mexico claimed the boundary was the Nueces River, north of the Rio Grande.

At the same time, Polk dispatched another agent, Thomas O. Larkin, to acquire California by quietly encouraging its Mexican and American residents to abandon Mexico and join the United States. Before these efforts were successful, a handful of Californians staged a revolt against Mexico and declared their independence, much the same way that Texans had done a decade earlier. The revolutionaries hoisted a crude flag with a bear on it, and the incident became known as the Bear Flag Revolt.

For a number of reasons, the Mexican government refused to receive Slidell, which ended his mission. Upon hearing that Slidell's mission had failed, Polk determined that war was necessary to acquire Mexico's provinces. But Polk sought to make the war look like it was started by Mexico. With tensions between the two nations mounting, Polk dispatched U.S. troops to the disputed area between the Rio Grande and the Nueces River. He claimed that the troops were still on American soil, but Mexico regarded the presence of American troops south of the Nueces as an invasion.

On May 9, 1846, Polk learned that Mexican troops had crossed the Rio Grande and ambushed an American patrol, killing or wounding sixteen men. The incident gave Polk the excuse he had been looking for to launch a military campaign to achieve the goals he had been unable to fulfill by peaceful means. On May 11, Polk read a war message to the U.S. Congress that clearly painted Mexico as the aggressor:

> But now, after reiterated menaces, Mexico has passed the boundary of the United States, has invaded our territory and shed American blood upon the American soil. She has proclaimed that hostilities have commenced, and that the two nations are now at war.

As war exists, and, notwithstanding all our efforts to avoid it, exists by the act of Mexico herself, we are called upon by every consideration of duty and patriotism to vindicate with decision the honor, the rights, and the interests of our country.[30]

Polk implored Congress to act promptly. Two days later, Congress declared war against Mexico.

By the summer of 1846, American troops occupied northern California, where they were joined by participants in the Bear Flag Revolt. Within days of their arrival, northern California was formally

The U.S. desire to acquire more land from Mexico resulted in a bloody war between the two nations. By 1848, the United States had reached its objective, annexing California and New Mexico from Mexico.

annexed to the United States. Southern California also fell to the Americans and was annexed. Far to the east, New Mexico was also occupied by American troops.

Although its objectives had been achieved, the U.S. launched an invasion of Mexico to humiliate Mexicans and their leader. On September 17, 1847, General Santa Anna, the man who had defeated Texans at the Alamo over a decade earlier, raised a white flag of surrender over Mexico City.

The surrender allowed the United States to dictate the terms of the peace treaty. American negotiators demanded that Mexico accept the Rio Grande as the border between Texas and Mexico. The negotiators bought all of California and New Mexico for $15,000,000. The U.S. government also assumed claims against the Mexican government totaling $3,250,000. With these major provisions set, the Treaty of Guadalupe Hidalgo was signed on February 2, 1848.

Securing the Oregon Territory

While the United States was at war with Mexico, the spirit of manifest destiny guided U. S. efforts to secure sole title to Oregon in the Pacific Northwest. This time the United States achieved its objective through settlement and diplomacy. Britain and the United States had signed a treaty of joint occupation in 1818 because the two nations could not agree on whose territory it was. The treaty was renewed for

The 49th Parallel

The Oregon Treaty established the 49th parallel as the boundary between Britain and the United States. The treaty was the final link in the creation of the present boundary between the United States and Canada. The text of the treaty appears in Documents of American History.

"From the point of the forty-ninth parallel of north latitude, where the boundary laid down in existing treaties and conventions between the United States and Great Britain terminates, the line of boundary between the territories of the United States and those of her Britannic Majesty shall be continued westward along the said forty-ninth parallel of north latitude to the middle of the channel which separates the continent from Vancouver's Island, and thence southerly through the middle of said channel, and of Fuca's Straits, to the Pacific Ocean; *provided, however,* That the navigation of the whole of the said channel and straits, south of the forty-ninth parallel of north latitude, remain free and open to both parties."

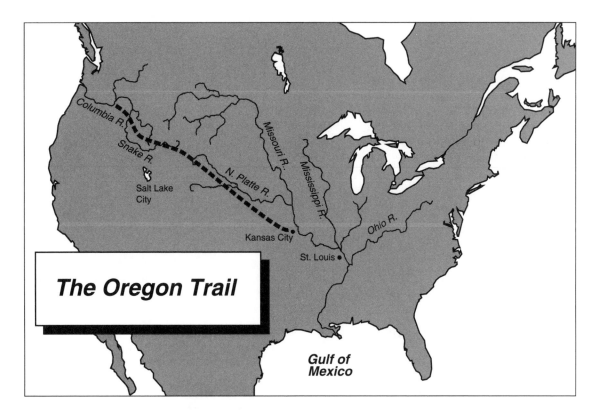

The Oregon Trail

the same reason in 1827. Throughout this period, British fur traders dominated the region. During the 1830s, however, a series of American ventures into Oregon challenged British domination.

Journals kept by early fur traders and government explorers inspired the earliest American efforts to settle Oregon. In March 1832, a Boston businessman named Nathaniel J. Wyeth led a small party across the Great Plains, over the mountains and deserts, finally reaching the Pacific Ocean. Wyeth's efforts to found a settlement failed, but the difficult route that he blazed later become famous as the Oregon Trail.

In 1840, Elijah White assembled a group of 120 men, which he led across the mountains in 1842. This party was the first large party to follow the overland route to Oregon. White's success was all that was needed to set Americans into motion. On May 22, 1843, a wagon train of 1,000 men, women, and children set out from Independence, Missouri, for Oregon in wagons. They took with them 7,500 oxen and cattle. The long wagon train arrived in the Willamette Valley of Oregon in late November.

This so-called Great Migration marked a turning point in Oregon history. Throughout the United States, Oregon became a household word, and more and more Americans dissatisfied with their eastern lives began making plans to head west. In 1845 alone, three thousand settlers made the trip over the Oregon Trail.

In his now famous inaugural address of March 4, 1845, President James K. Polk ignored the joint treaty with Britain and claimed title to Oregon. He linked its settlement to an American tradition of expansion, and predicted that it would soon become a part of the United States.

> Our title to the country of Oregon is "clear and unquestionable" and already are our people preparing to perfect that title by occupying it with their wives and children. But eighty years ago our population was confined on the west by the ridge of the Alleghenies. Within that period—within the lifetime, I might say, of some of my hearers—our people, increasing to many millions, have filled the eastern valley of the Mississippi, adventurously ascended the Missouri to its headsprings, and are already engaged in establishing the blessings of self-government in valleys of which the rivers flow to the Pacific. . . . The increasing facilities of intercourse will easily bring the States, of which the formation in that part of our territory can not be long delayed, within the sphere of our federative Union.[31]

By the end of 1845, 5,000 Americans were living in Oregon, compared to only 750 Britons. British leaders realized that American control of Oregon was inevitable. The timing was right for a permanent boundary to be drawn between

A wagon train of settlers moves west along the Oregon Trail. The difficult route took travelers across the Great Plains, over rugged mountains, and through vast desert areas.

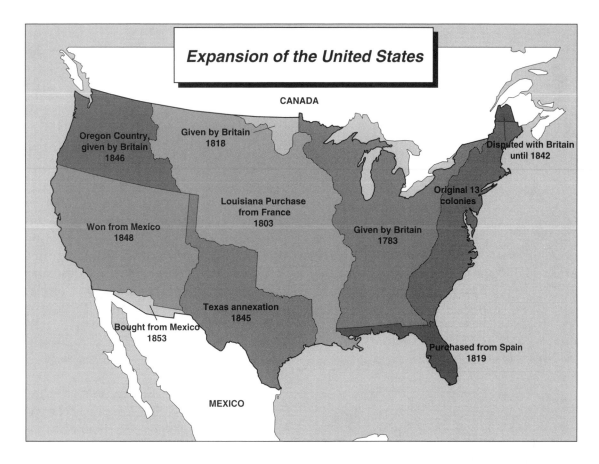

Expansion of the United States

CANADA

Oregon Country, given by Britain 1846

Given by Britain 1818

Disputed with Britain until 1842

Louisiana Purchase from France 1803

Original 13 colonies

Won from Mexico 1848

Given by Britain 1783

Texas annexation 1845

Bought from Mexico 1853

Purchased from Spain 1819

MEXICO

American and British interests in Oregon. The question, of course, was where to draw the boundary. Neither country wanted to go to war over it. As the 49th parallel already formed the border between the two nations east of the Rocky Mountains, it was agreed to extend it to the Pacific. Primary U.S. interests were south of the 49th parallel, and British interests lay north of that line, so the compromise was acceptable to both countries. On June 15, 1846, a new treaty was signed that extended the 49th parallel across the Rocky Mountains to the Pacific Ocean. This treaty gave a large portion of Oregon to the United States, and established the final link in the long boundary between the United States and Canada that exists today.

Through settlement, diplomacy, and warfare, the United States had fulfilled its manifest destiny and reached the Pacific Ocean. The acquisitions of Texas, Oregon, New Mexico, and California added 1,200,000 square miles to the United States, and established its present continental borders. But much of this land, along with other U. S. lands west of the Mississippi River, remained unsettled wilderness. During the next half century, the frontier would continue to lure millions of Americans in search of opportunity.

Chapter

6 Transforming the West

In 1848 most of the vast territory between the Mississippi River and the Pacific Ocean was wilderness. Millions of Americans soon heeded the advice made famous by *New York Tribune* editor Horace Greeley. "Go West, young man," Greeley wrote,

After the discovery of gold in California, would-be prospectors rushed from all over the country to seek their fortune on the west coast.

"and grow up with the country."[32] In the mid-1800s, Americans were lured west by three growing industries. Mining promised fortunes in the form of gold and silver. Cattle ranching offered high profits to visionary ranchers. Agriculture gave farmers yet another chance to claim free land as their own. These three great ventures often overlapped each other in both geography and time.

Those who exploited these economic frontiers continued to displace Native Americans in their quest for prosperity: By the end of the century Americans had transformed the west from wilderness into states and organized territories dotted with ranches, farms, towns, and cities, and only traces of native cultures remained.

The Mining Frontier

On January 24, 1848, James Marshall was at work building a sawmill for John A. Sutter on the banks of the American River in central California. Marshall noticed several yellow nuggets lying in the mill trace, a wooden trough through which the water ran. Marshall had discovered what became known as the Mother Lode, the richest gold deposits the nation would ever see.

John Sutter's mill, the site of the gold discovery that would start California's gold rush.

Not until August 1848 did the first reports of the gold strike reach the east. At that point, the nation was stricken with gold fever. On January 16, 1849, the *New York Herald* reported that all over the United States, would-be prospectors were

> rushing head over heels towards the El Dorado on the Pacific—that wonderful California, which sets the public mind almost on the highway to insanity. . . . Every day, men of property and means are advertising their possessions for sale, in order to furnish them with the means to reach that golden land.[33]

Those who hurried to "that golden land" were nicknamed "Forty-niners."

The first miners lived in the wilderness next to their claims, and were self-reliant out of necessity. But the rush of gold seekers quickly transformed the wilderness around them. Towns with names like An-

gel's Camp, Dutch Flat, and Grass Valley sprang up almost overnight. As mining towns sprang up, many miners discouraged by hard work and low yields soon returned to their former professions as small tradesmen, mechanics, store-keepers, gamblers, hotel keepers, lawyers. In a few short years, some sections of the Mother Lode were as developed as many eastern regions.

For most gold seekers, the anticipated fortunes never materialized. Those miners lucky enough to strike it rich reaped a share of the greatest gold strike in American history. In 1852, for example, the Mother Lode yielded an estimated $81,249,700 in gold, and by 1900, $1,300,000,000.

The Mother Lode was the first of several great mining frontiers that helped open the west. Both gold and silver were discovered in Nevada in 1858, and by the following year, a new fever gripped the

Prospecting

Mark Twain described the tedious process of prospecting for gold and silver on the mining frontier in Roughing It, *first published in 1871.*

"Day after day we toiled, and climbed, and searched, and we younger partners grew sicker and still sicker of the promiseless toil. At last we halted under a beetling rampart of rock which projected from the earth high upon the mountain. Mr. Ballou broke off some fragments with a hammer, and examined them long and attentively with a small eyeglass; threw them away and broke off more; said this rock was quartz, and quartz was the sort of rock that contained silver. *Contained* it! I had thought that at least it would be caked on the outside of it like a kind of veneering. He still broke off pieces and critically examined them, now and then wetting the piece with his tongue and applying the glass. At last he exclaimed:

'We've got it!'

We were full of anxiety in a moment. The rock was clean and white, where it was broken, and across it ran a ragged thread of blue. He said that that little thread had silver in it, mixed with base metals, such as lead and antimony, and other rubbish, and that there was a speck or two of gold visible. After a great deal of effort we managed to discern some fine yellow specks, and judged that a couple of tons of them massed together might make a gold dollar, possibly."

nation. Miners nicknamed "Fifty-niners" rushed to Nevada. The rich deposits of gold and silver there became known as the Comstock Lode.

Carson City quickly became the hub of the Comstock region. Like other mining towns, it sprang up almost overnight. When writer Samuel Clemens visited Carson City in the early 1860s, it was a thriving town, typical of many gold rush communities. Clemens described Carson City under his pseudonym, Mark Twain, in *Roughing It*, first published in 1871:

It was a "wooden" town; its population two thousand souls. The main street consisted of four or five blocks of white frame stores . . . [which] were packed close together, side by side, as if room were scarce in that mighty plain. The sidewalk was of boards that were more or less loose and inclined to rattle when walked upon. In the middle of the town, opposite the stores, was the "plaza" which is native to all towns beyond the Rocky Mountains—a large, unfenced, level vacancy, with a liberty pole in it, and very useful as a place for public auctions, horse trades, and mass meetings, and likewise for teamsters to camp in. Two other sides of the plaza were faced by stores, offices, and stables. The rest of Carson City was pretty scattering.[34]

While the Mother Lode and Comstock continued to draw miners to California and Nevada, newly discovered deposits of gold, silver, and other metals opened up other parts of the west. Gold and silver in some quantity was eventually found in every state west of the Great Plains. Colorado experienced an economic boom when gold, silver, and lead mining flourished there between 1859 and 1880. The last great mining frontier opened in 1877, when gold was discovered in the Black Hills of the Dakota Territory.

Mining sped up settlement and development in the west. The first settlers in many areas of the west were miners hoping to strike it rich. They were soon followed by thousands of others, which dramatically

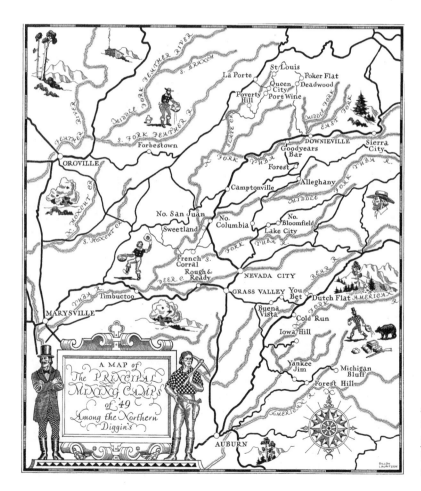

An early-twentieth-century map shows the sites of principal mining camps in the west during the 1849 gold rush.

speeded migration from the east. Census records for California illustrate gold's impact on the dramatic growth in population. At the close of 1848, California claimed 14,000 residents in the category "other than Indians." By the end of 1849, nearly 100,000 Forty-niners had journeyed to California's goldfields. Three years later, the population reached 250,000, and by 1860, it had increased to 360,000.

The entry of western states into the Union also shows how mining accelerated western development. California became a state in 1850, nine years before Oregon, which had no significant mining booms. Nevada entered the Union in 1864 and Colorado in 1876. Situated between those two states, the non–gold rush territory of Utah did not join the Union until 1896.

Mining brought the first waves of Americans to open the west. Many of the gold seekers had crossed the Great Plains on their way west, traveling through the homelands of numerous Native American nations. Because they were only passing through, the gold seekers encountered minimal trouble. But when cattle ranchers and farmers began to establish permanent

Gold miners pan for gold in a California town. The mining frontier played a crucial role in the settlement of California.

In addition to California, miners flocked to Nevada and Colorado (pictured) when gold and other metals were discovered there.

settlements on the Great Plains, Native Americans rose up in resistance. Once again advancing settlers and Native Americans engaged in a long and bitter struggle for control of the frontier.

A Bitter Conflict

The majority of settlers regarded Native Americans of the Great Plains as savages, inferiors whose presence formed a barrier to settlement. As it had in the past, the U.S. government amended its policies to fit changing situations, but its goal always remained the same—to remove the native barrier and open the land for settlers. The bitter forty-year conflict between American settlers and the Dakotas, a confederation of native nations on the northern Great Plains, is characteristic of the cultural clashes that occurred during a generation of turbulence on the Great Plains.

The conflict began as early as 1851, when four Minnesota bands of Dakotas ceded 24 million acres of land in southern Minnesota to the United States for a little over $3 million. The Dakotas subsisted on a narrow reservation straddling

"The Indians must be thoroughly whipped"

Albert Barnitz, a lieutenant in Custer's 7th Cavalry, was pessimistic about the Peace Commission's policies. In a letter to his wife, Jennie, reprinted in The American Frontier, *he favored "whipping" Native Americans. The 7th Cavalry was annihilated at the Little Big Horn in 1876, nine years after Barnitz composed this letter.*

"Aug. 13, 1867

. . . We are to have peace soon, it seems!—Genl. Sherman, and the Peace Commissioners have met, and decided upon it, it appears, and the big councils are to be held up on the Platte in the full moon of September and at Larned in the full moon of October, and the presents will be distributed, and the new guns, and everything, and then we will go into winter quarters before Christmas, and in the Spring we will repeat the pleasant little farce of a Big Indian War, and a hand-full of men to carry it on.

Of course the peace won't amount to any thing, except that it will enable the Commissioners to distribute presents!—But may be some more extensive preparations will be made for the next war. The Indians must be thoroughly whipped before they will respect us, or keep any peace, and they haven't been whipped very much to speak of."

the Minnesota River. In 1858, the Dakotas were pressured into ceding lands north of the Minnesota River to the government, reducing their reservation to a narrow strip of land along the river's southern bank.

Deprived of their nomadic lifestyle, the Dakotas were forced to depend on annuities and supplies from the U.S. government. When their government payments were repeatedly delayed, the hungry Dakotas became restless and angry. On August 17, 1862, a mission by four Dakota braves to steal eggs from a settler's farm near Acton, Minnesota, took a tragic turn when one brave challenged another's courage and the other pledged to kill a settler. Before the four left the farm, five settlers had been killed.

The incident set the Minnesota frontier aflame. The Dakotas launched an all-out effort to drive settlers from their old lands. In attacks over the next few weeks, the Dakotas killed an estimated five hundred settlers. Their own losses were much lower, as few as twenty-six killed. The rebellion was soon put down by Minnesota regiments. More than three hundred Dakotas were charged with crimes stemming from the rebellion and sentenced to death. President Abraham Lincoln personally reviewed the cases and commuted the sentences of most of the condemned. But on December 26, 1862, thirty-eight

Dakotas were hanged at Mankato, in Minnesota, the largest public execution in U.S. history.

A new phase of the Dakota conflict began in Montana four years later. To connect the mining town of Bozeman with the east, the U.S. government began to survey a road through the Big Horn Mountains, the favorite Dakota hunting grounds. All through 1866, the Dakotas harassed soldiers as they worked on the road. In December of that year, they ambushed a party led by Capt. W. J. Fetterman, killing all eighty-two of its members.

The incident led the American government to reevaluate its Native American policy. The Peace Commission was set up to address all the Native American problems across the Great Plains. For years, the government had let the Dakotas and other Native American nations roam and hunt on the Great Plains almost as they pleased. In effect, the U.S. government treated the northern Great Plains as one big reservation upon which the Native Americans were allowed to live. In the wake of the Montana incident, the Peace Commission recommended that the government replace its one-big-reservation policy with the concept of small reservations. To the Peace Commission, the idea of small reservations was, Ray Allen Billington writes, echoing the language and attitudes of the times,

the only workable solution to the West's racial problem. Red men must be segregated at isolated points where, as wards of the government, they could be taught to live in fixed homes, till the soil, and begin a transition to civilized ways which would culminate when they could be assimilated as ordinary citizens. Both expansionist westerners and humanitarian easterners would certainly approve. Frontiersmen would be satisfied because sedentary tribesmen required less

After the Dakotas killed hundreds of settlers in an attempt to drive settlers from Native American land, thirty-eight members of the tribe were executed by the U.S. government for their role in the rebellion.

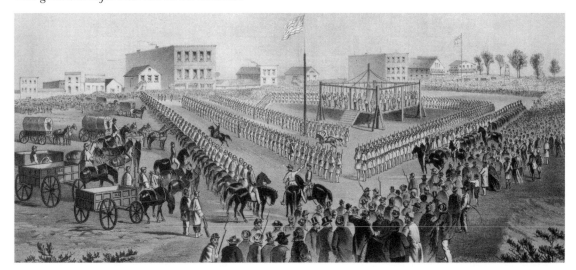

space than hunters, releasing thousands of acres for settlement.[35]

On April 29, 1868, the U.S. government and the Dakotas signed a treaty that created a permanent reservation in Dakota territory west of the Missouri River. The Dakotas were allowed the use of their old hunting grounds until they were wanted by the United States. The country just east of the Big Horns was recognized as unceded Dakota territory. In turn, the government agreed to abandon the road it was constructing through the Dakota's hunting grounds.

The treaty was only a temporary solution to the conflict. In 1875, the U.S. government attempted to force the Dakotas to abandon their hunting grounds east of the Little Big Horn and accept life on a reservation. The Dakotas rebelled.

A military expedition against the Dakotas was launched in the spring of 1876. Among its officers was a flamboyant, reckless general named George Armstrong Custer. On June 25, 1876, Custer's force of 265 men encountered what Custer took to be a small Dakota camp. In fact, Custer had stumbled upon the Dakota's main headquarters, which held 2,500 warriors. Custer's forces were quickly surrounded and within several hours all were killed.

(Left) About to face his death, General George Custer stands among his men during the battle against the Dakotas. (Right) A photograph from about 1865 portrays the flamboyant and often arrogant Custer.

Cattle ranchers load cattle onto a train in Kansas for shipment to eastern markets.

The Dakotas, however, had no time to celebrate their victory. Other U.S. forces slowly drove them toward the east. In October, three thousand Dakotas were caught in an army trap. Some escaped to Canada, but most surrendered and returned to their reservation.

The defeat marked the last great battle between the Dakotas and whites on the Great Plains. The struggle for the northern Great Plains represents one of the saddest chapters in America's frontier history. Unfortunately, it was not the only such conflict between Native Americans and advancing settlers. At the same time that the U.S. government fought the Dakotas for control of the northern Great Plains, it carried out similar campaigns against Native Americans on the southern Great Plains. In virtually every part of the west, settlers and the U.S. government clashed with Native Americans during the opening of the west. In every conflict, the results ended with the defeat of the Native Americans.

The Cattle Frontier

The end of Native American resistance made the Great Plains safe for the opening of another economic venture that helped to transform the west. Beginning in the 1860s, visionary ranchers took advantage of open land to establish a brief but impressive cattle empire on the Great Plains.

Cattle ranching was not new to the west. Small cattle ranchers had herded cattle on the Texas plains since the days of Spanish rule. But the Texas cattle industry never flourished because it was nearly impossible to get cattle to eastern markets, where they could be slaughtered and processed for consumption. The construction of the transcontinental railroad across the Great Plains to connect the east with the mining frontiers in California and Nevada made it easier for ranchers to connect with eastern markets. All the cattle ranchers had to do was drive their herds north to the rail lines and ship their cattle east by rail.

In March of 1866 ranchers organized the first "Long Drive" from the plains of Texas north to the railhead at Sedalia, Missouri. The drive was plagued by bad weather and resistance from Missouri farmers who did not want disease-infected Texas cattle contaminating their own herds. Nevertheless, enough cattle made it to Sedalia to convince ranchers that the Long Drive would work if a better railhead could be established.

In 1867, an Illinois meat dealer named Joseph M. McCoy transformed the isolated hamlet of Abilene, Kansas, into a railhead. Almost overnight, the cattle industry was born. Between 1868 and 1871, nearly 1,500,000 cattle were driven from the Texas range north to Abilene and shipped east.

McCoy had ample opportunity to observe the cattle drovers, or cowboys, who

The cattle empire of the Great Plains helped to transform the west, bringing prosperity and more settlers to the land.

"A dreary, dreary life"

These verses from "Cowboy's Life," a popular song, paint an alternative portrait of the lifestyle of the much-romanticized American cowboy. The song is reprinted in volume 10 of Annals of America.

"A cowboy's life is a dreary, dreary life;
Some say it's free from care,
Rounding up the cattle from morning till night,
On the bald prairie so bare.

Just about four o'clock old cook will holler out,
'Roll out, boys, it's almost day.'
Through his broken slumbers the puncher he will ask,
'Has the short summer night passed away?'

The cowboy's life is a dreary, dreary life,
He's driven through the heat and cold
While the rich man's a-sleeping on his velvet couch,
Dreaming of silver and gold.

When the spring work sets in, then our troubles will begin,
The weather being fierce and cold;
We're almost froze, with the water in our clothes,
And the cattle we can scarcely hold."

Contrary to their romanticized image, frontier cowboys often led a lonely, wearisome life.

herded the cattle across the plains. He found cowboys to be "mostly honorable men" who, he observed, were always chivalrously courteous to a modest lady; possessing a strong, innate sense of right and wrong, a quick, impulsive temper, great lovers of a horse and always good riders and good horsemen; always free to spend their money lavishly for such objects or purposes as best please them; very quick to detect an injury or insult, and not slow to avenge it nor quick to forget it; always ready to help a comrade out of a scrape, full of life and fun; would illy brook rules of restraint, free and easy.[36]

McCoy's description of the cowboy captured essential elements of the American character that had evolved during the nation's history. More than any other figure, the cowboy has become fixed in the mind of Americans as a symbol of the American character. Even today, many Americans admire the cowboy's philosophy and imitate his dress.

The high profits of the cattle industry attracted thousands of ranchers and speculators from the east and as far away as Europe, all eager to make fortunes on the open range. The rush of men and money to the cattle frontier proved to be a factor in its decline. By 1885, the Great Plains were overpopulated with cattle, and profits were falling. The bitter winter of 1886–87 killed thousands of cattle, forcing many cattle companies into bankruptcy. The cattle industry collapsed and plunged into an economic decline from which it never recovered.

But even had the cattle industry not suffered economic collapse, its days were numbered. The open land that ranchers depended upon was already disappearing as increasing numbers of farmers began carving farms out of the Great Plains. The cattlemen, who had helped open the Great Plains to settlement, gave way to the farmers.

The Agricultural Frontier

As in earlier American frontiers, it was farmers, the last in the line of frontiersmen, who truly conquered the west. Dissatisfied by conditions at home, lured by the promise of free land, and aided by new technology, they came by the thousands to the Great Plains beginning in the 1850s.

As pioneers of the Great Lakes agricultural frontier had done, Great Plains farmers learned new pioneering techniques to claim the semiarid land. Their efforts were greatly aided by rapid advances in technology after the Civil War. The rise of eastern factories made it possible for new plows and improved hay and grain harvesting equipment to be mass produced, making them available to thousands of pioneers for the first time.

The most significant innovation to transform the west was barbed wire. The first Great Plains farmers quickly found they needed fences to keep range cattle out of their newly planted crops. But farmers found little stone or wood on the Great Plains with which to build fences. Then a DeKalb, Illinois, farmer named Joseph F. Glidden invented barbed wire, and began manufacturing it in 1874. Barbed wire revolutionized fencing. Farmers bought it by the mile and fenced off millions of acres from trespassing livestock.

It took more than technology, however, to lure farmers west. To encourage settlers to move west, and to help them get started, Congress passed the Homestead Act in 1862. The Homestead Act allowed settlers to claim up to 160 acres of free land from the public domain by settling on it and making required improve-

"There was nothing but land"

In her classic pioneer novel My Antonia, *Willa Cather recalled her own first impressions of the prairies of Nebraska through the eyes of the story's narrator, Jim Burton. Thousands of Americans and immigrants from other countries made similar trips to the agricultural frontier on the Great Plains.*

"I rode in the straw in the bottom of the wagon-box, covered up with a buffalo hide. The immigrants rumbled off into the empty darkness, and we followed them.

I tried to go to sleep, but the jolting made me bite my tongue, and I soon began to ache all over. When the straw settled down, I had a hard bed. Cautiously I slipped from under the buffalo hide, got up on my knees and peered over the side of the wagon. There seemed to be nothing to see; no fences, no creeks or trees, no hills or fields. If there was a road, I could not make it out in the faint starlight. There was nothing but land: not a country at all, but the material out of which countries are made. No, there was nothing but land—slightly undulating, I knew, because often our wheels ground against the brake as we went down into a hollow and lurched up again on the other side. I had the feeling that the world was left behind, that we had got over the edge of it, and were outside man's jurisdiction. I had never before looked up at the sky when there was not a familiar mountain ridge against it. But this was the complete dome of heaven, all there was of it. . . . The wagon jolted on, carrying me I knew not whither."

---

ments over a five-year period. In 1873, Congress also passed the Timber Culture Act, which granted farmers an additional 160 acres of land if they planted a portion of it in trees.

Although the acts were intended to aid small-scale farmers and factory laborers who had little savings, they were widely abused by profit-minded land speculators. As little as one acre of every nine given away by the government actually went to the government's intended beneficiaries.

Despite these abuses, the land acts served as a powerful advertising tool for the Great Plains. Some settlers came from the Mississippi Valley, where conditions were crowded. Others emigrated from Europe, drawn by newspaper advertisements so filled with misleading promises of prosperity that they bordered on the fraudulent.

Instead of finding immediate prosperity, settlers frequently endured severe hardship upon their arrival. Often they lived in the most primitive conditions, building barns and outbuildings even before they built their own homes. In the novel *My Antonia*, Willa Cather recalled her own pioneer experiences when she described the cavelike dugout of the Shimerdas, an immigrant Bohemian family that settled the Nebraska prairie:

As we approached the Shimerdas' dwelling, I could still see nothing but rough red hillocks, and draws with shelving banks and long roots hanging out where the earth had crumbled away. Presently, against one of those banks, I saw a sort of shed, thatched with the same wine-coloured grass that grew everywhere else. Near it tilted a

An advertisement beckons settlers to Iowa and Nebraska with promises of unlimited land.

shattered windmill frame, that had no wheel. We drove up to this shelter to tie our horses, and then I saw a door and window sunk deep in the drawbank. The door stood open, and a woman and a girl of fourteen ran out and looked at us hopefully. A little girl trailed along behind them.[37]

To prove their claims, farmers battled plagues of grasshoppers that stripped the land of all vegetation. They endured prairie fires that reduced the landscape to ashes and bitter winter blizzards that isolated them for weeks.

But farmers triumphed over these and other hardships and transformed the Great Plains from open prairie into fertile farms. By 1890, farmers had claimed more than 430 million acres of land on the Great Plains, more land than all of their ancestors had claimed throughout American history.

The taming of the Great Plains by farmers was only part of the incredible transformation of the west. In less than half a century, farmers, miners, cattle ranchers, and millions of others who followed them west had made the wilderness an integral part of the United States.

Excluding the states of Missouri and Arkansas, only 398,000 people lived west of the Mississippi in 1850. By 1890, the area west of the Mississippi had been divided into fourteen states and four territories. According to U.S. census figures for that year, the combined population of these states and territories was 8,525,000 people, 13.5 percent of the nation's total population.

Two years after the 1890 census was completed, the U.S. government published a compendium of national statistics. While

The Oklahoma Land Rush

On April 22, 1889, fifty thousand land-hungry settlers took up positions near the Oklahoma border waiting for the starting signal that would let them enter Oklahoma to claim land newly opened for settlement. Participant Hamilton S. Wicks recorded these observations, which appeared in volume 11 of the Annals of America.

"Suddenly the air was pierced with the blast of a bugle. Hundreds of throats echoed the sound with shouts of exultation. The quivering limbs of saddled steeds, no longer restrained by the hands that held their bridles, bounded forward simultaneously into the 'beautiful land' of Oklahoma; and wagons and carriages and buggies and prairie schooners and a whole congregation of curious equipages joined in this unparalleled race, where every starter was bound to win a prize—the 'Realization States' of home and prosperity. . . . Away dashed the thoroughbreds, the broncos, the pintos, and the mustangs at a breakneck pace across the uneven surface of the prairie. It was amazing to witness the recklessness of those cowboy riders. They jumped obstacles, they leaped ditches; they cantered with no diminution of speed through water pools; and when they came to a ravine too wide to leap, down they would go with a rush, and up the other side with a spurt of energy, to scurry once more like mad over the level plain. . . .

The race was not over when you reached the particular lot you were content to select for your possession. The contest still was who should drive their stakes first, who would erect their little tents soonest, and then, who would quickest build a wooden shanty."

reviewing a copy of this volume, a young historian named Frederick Jackson Turner read this short statement: "Up to and including 1880 the country had a frontier of settlement, but at present the unsettled area has been so broken into by isolated bodies of settlement that there can hardly be said to be a frontier line. In discussion of its extent, its westward movement etc., it can not, therefore, any longer have a place in census reports."[38] Turner immediately recognized that an era had come to an end. His study of the frontier's significance would help rewrite American history.

7 The Frontier's Significance

At the time that the *Compendium of the Eleventh Census* announced that the frontier no longer had a place in census reports, no one had yet interpreted its role in shaping the development of America and the character of Americans. A few

American historian Frederick Jackson Turner promoted the idea that the frontier played a primary role in American development.

commentators, such as Alexis de Tocqueville, had recognized that the "boundless continent" had helped to shape the nation. The majority of scholars, however, linked American development to the nation's origins in Europe.

The importance of the frontier as a primary force in American development was first recognized by Frederick Jackson Turner, a young American historian from Wisconsin who was himself raised on the frontier. Turner's observations not only explained the role of the frontier but revolutionized the study of American history.

Turner introduced his frontier hypothesis in a paper he presented at a meeting of the American Historical Association held in Chicago on July 2, 1893. The paper, which Turner titled "The Significance of the Frontier in American History," was published in the *Proceedings of the State Historical Society of Wisconsin* at the end of that year.

Turner began by quoting the passage from *Compendium of the Eleventh Census* announcing the deletion of the frontier category from the census report. Then he explained the extraordinary significance of the deletion:

> This brief official statement marks the closing of a great historical movement. Up to our own day American history

Distinctive Traits

In America's Frontier Heritage, *Ray Allen Billington expanded on Frederick Jackson Turner's list of American characteristics influenced by the frontier.*

"Their faith in democratic institutions, their belief in equality, their insistence that class lines shall never hinder social mobility, their wasteful economy, their unwillingness to admit that automation has lessened the need for hard work, their lack of attachment to place, their eagerness to experiment and to favor the new over the old, all mark the people of the United States as unique. To say that these characteristics and attitudes were solely the result of a pioneering past is to ignore many other forces that have helped shape the American character. But to deny that three centuries of frontiering endowed the people with some of their most distinctive traits is to neglect a basic molding force that has been the source of the nation's greatest strength—and some of its most regrettable weaknesses."

has been in a large degree the history of the colonization of the Great West. The existence of an area of free land, its continuous recession, and the advance of American settlement westward, explain American development. . . . American social development has been continually beginning over again on the frontier. This perennial rebirth, this fluidity of American life, this expansion westward with its new opportunities, its continuous touch with the simplicity of primitive society, furnish the forces dominating American character. The true point of view in the history of this nation is not the Atlantic coast, it is the Great West.[39]

With this observation Turner opened a new era in the study of American history. Instead of looking to the Atlantic coast and Europe for answers about the origins of American attitudes, values, and institutions, Turner and many historians who followed in his footsteps turned toward the frontier.

Defining the Frontier

Beginning with the Atlantic coast, Turner identified many geographic frontiers as American settlement moved from east to west across the continent. He explained how the frontier originated on the Atlantic coast, crossed the Allegheny Mountains into the Ohio Valley, then moved across the Mississippi River, eventually extending all the way to the Pacific coast.

Turner outlined many similarities in this succession of geographic frontiers:

> Each was won by a series of Indian wars. . . . The first frontier had to meet its Indian question, its question of the disposition of the public domain, of the means of intercourse with older settlements, of the extension of political organization, of religious and educational activity. And the settlement of these and similar questions for one frontier served as a guide for the next.[40]

Within each of these geographic frontiers, Turner observed a repeating pattern in the waves of settlers and the order of settlement:

> Stand at the Cumberland Gap and watch the procession of civilization, marching single file—the buffalo following the trail to the salt springs, the Indian, fur-trader and hunter, the cattle-raiser, the pioneer farmer—and the frontier has passed by. Stand at South Pass in the Rockies a century later and see the same procession with wider intervals between.[41]

Turner divided this procession of settlers marching across the wilderness into a series of frontiers, moving one by one across

The mining frontier was one of the many frontiers, according to Turner, that helped shape American attitudes, values, and institutions.

each geographic frontier, which he called the trader's frontier, the rancher's frontier, the miner's frontier, and the farmer's frontier.

Explaining the Frontier's Significance

After studying and comparing the various kinds of frontiers and the way they advanced across the continent, Turner was able to draw a number of conclusions about the frontier's significance in American development. First, Turner recognized that the frontier helped create a composite American nationality. The frontier placed English settlers alongside settlers of many other nationalities. As these settlers shared ideas with each other through the years, a unique American nationality developed that was a composite of all.

The isolation of the frontier helped to reinforce this new American nationality. As the frontier moved farther west, English influence decreased. For example, frontier residents were forced to manufacture their own goods because it became too difficult to get goods from England. As their independence grew, Americans identified less and less with England.

Turner also believed that laws that helped build the nation responded to the needs of the frontier. Much of this legislation centered around the distribution of land in the public domain. The Ordinance of 1787, for example, created the mechanism that allowed new territories to be organized and later admitted into the Union, allowing the United States to grow.

This measure also influenced the nation in another way. The need to find a way to transfer land in the public domain to private individuals raised questions about the power of the U.S. government as defined by the Constitution. To satisfy the needs of the frontier, government leaders interpreted the Constitution more loosely. This helped to expand the duties of the national government. As a result of the Ordinance of 1787 and other legislation, the national government became more powerful.

The Frontier Promoted Democracy

Although the frontier played an important role in creating an American nationality and securing landmark legislation, it played an even more significant role in the evolution of democracy, in part through its tradition of individualism. On the frontier, individualism was valued over a strong government because people disliked having government telling them what to do. Dislike of government motivated frontier residents to keep the government in the hands of many people, rather than allowing it to be controlled by only a few. Another way that the frontier promoted democracy was through suffrage, or right to vote, provisions. Frontier governments were quicker than eastern governments to relax voting requirements for men. Because frontier governments made it easier for men to vote, eastern governments were soon forced to do the same. As a result, more Americans were able to participate in the government, making it more democratic. Because the frontier encouraged individualism and expanded suffrage, Turner concluded that

Settlers clear land to establish a homestead. The settlement of the American frontier brought out an independent spirit in its residents, one of the traits that would forever shape the American character.

the "most important effect of the frontier has been in the promotion of democracy here and in Europe."[42]

But there was also danger in the democracy promoted by the frontier. Alexis de Tocqueville, for example, had seen that the "tyranny of the majority" often ignored the rights of minorities. The frontier also seemed to breed periods of economic chaos in America. Turner studied several such periods and found that they coincided in place and time with the opening of new frontiers. He concluded that

> the democracy born of free land, strong in selfishness and individualism, intolerant of administrative experience and education, and pressing individual liberty beyond its proper bounds, has its dangers as well as its

benefits. Individualism in America has allowed a laxity in regard to governmental affairs which has rendered possible the spoils system and all the manifest evils that follow from the lack of a highly developed civic spirit.[43]

The Frontier Shaped the American Character

Turner concluded his analysis of the American frontier's significance with some observations about the frontier's influence in forming the character of Americans. He observed that as early as colonial times, foreigners traveling on the American frontier recognized "certain common traits," among frontier residents, which persisted even when civilization conquered the frontier:

> [T]o the frontier the American intellect owes its striking characteristics. That coarseness and strength combined with acuteness and inquisitiveness; that practical, inventive turn of mind, quick to find expedients; that masterful grasp of material things, lacking in the artistic but powerful to effect great ends; that restless, nervous energy; that dominant individualism, working for good and for evil, and withal that buoyancy and exuberance which comes with freedom—these are traits of the frontier, or traits called out elsewhere because of the existence of the frontier.[44]

Turner's hypothesis emphasized the way the frontier had influenced American development by promoting nationalism, influencing legislation, promoting democracy, and helping to shape the American character. In formulating his hypothesis, Turner made no predictions about the nation's future. But he clearly understood that a frontierless America would necessarily be different. "And now, four centuries from the discovery of America, at the end of a hundred years of life under the Constitution, the frontier has gone," he concluded, "and with its going has closed the first period of American history."[45]

The Impact of the Closing of the Frontier

In the more than one hundred years since the frontier closed, historians continue to study the impact its closing has had on America and Americans. In many ways, the official closing of the frontier was merely a formality, acknowledged by few people. Although there was no longer an advancing line of settlement, millions of acres in the west remained unclaimed and the frontiering process continued. Homesteaders claimed free land well into the early 1900s. When free land finally disappeared in America, some homesteaders moved to Canada.

During this period, the final steps of the three-hundred-year process of building the nation took place. Oklahoma was admitted to the Union in 1907, followed by Arizona and New Mexico in 1912. The entry of these three states created the forty-eight contiguous states that exist today. (Alaska, north of the forty-eight contiguous states, purchased from Russia in 1864, and the Hawaiian Islands in the Pacific Ocean, annexed in 1898, would be admitted as the forty-ninth and fiftieth states, respectively, in 1959.)

Since its days as a British colony, America had been a rural, agrarian society. As the availability of free land declined, however, the nation's population began to shift. Instead of continuously moving west to seek opportunity, people began to flock toward the nation's cities, where factories offered them jobs. By 1910, America was becoming a nation of cities and factories.

Some historians argue that the closing of the frontier also changed the role of the U.S. government, for example in providing "opportunity" for Americans.

Since the early years of the twentieth century, Americans have lived in a "closed society" with no frontier. Some historians argue that the financial aid provided to Americans by the U.S. government has

No Place to Go

In The Red Pony, *John Steinbeck's classic novel set in the early 1900s, Grandfather explains the real importance of "westering" to his young grandson, Jody. In this disarmingly simple scene, Steinbeck explores the psychological impact on the American character of westering and the subsequent closing of the American frontier.*

"Jody hardly knew when Grandfather started to talk. 'I shouldn't stay here, feeling the way I do.' He examined his strong old hands. 'I feel as though the crossing wasn't worth doing.' His eyes moved up the side-hill and stopped on a motionless hawk perched on a dead limb. 'I tell those old stories, but they're not what I want to tell. I only know how I want people to feel when I tell them.

'It wasn't Indians that were important, nor adventures, nor even getting out here. It was a whole bunch of people made into one big crawling beast. And I was the head. It was westering and westering. Every man wanted something for himself, but the big beast that was all of them wanted only westering. I was the leader, but if I hadn't been there, someone else would have been the head. The thing had to have a head. . . .

'We carried life out here and set it down the way those ants carry eggs. And I was the leader. The westering was as big as God, and the slow steps that made the movement piled up and piled up until the continent was crossed.

'Then we came down to the sea, and it was done.' He stopped and wiped his eyes until the rims were red. 'That's what I should be telling instead of stories.'

When Jody spoke, Grandfather started and looked down at him. 'Maybe I could lead the people some day,' Jody said.

The old man smiled. 'There's no place to go. There's the ocean to stop you. There's a line of old men along the shore hating the ocean because it stopped them.'"

slowly become a substitute for the opportunities once provided by the frontier. In the 1930s, for example, Franklin D. Roosevelt promised a "New Deal" to provide opportunites for Americans. During Roosevelt's presidency, government aid programs such as Social Security and welfare were created to fulfill the economic needs of Americans. These types of programs attempted "to secure for the individuals through positive governmental action the social welfare and economic opportunity that was once provided by free land."[46] By studying these and other changes in America during the twentieth century, historians have been able to deepen their insight into the frontier's significance and its impact on America during the nation's building years.

Challenging the Frontier Hypothesis

Some historians have reevaluated the continuing significance of Turner's frontier hypothesis. In 1929, years of economic prosperity suddenly ended with the crash of the stock market in New York City. The nation was plunged into an economic depression. Historians searched the past for clues to the cause of the depression. Turner's hypothesis failed to give them the answers they sought. The hypothesis, once considered the key to America's past, was challenged by numerous historians, partly because it could not adequately help them explain the present.

Turner clearly intended his hypothesis to summarize the frontier era, rather than apply to the future. But despite the loss of universal acceptance, Turner's frontier hypothesis remains an important and respected concept in the study of history. In 1951, for example, historian Walter

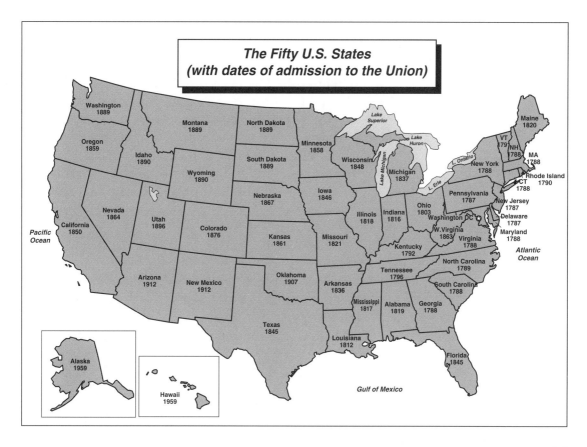

The Fifty U.S. States (with dates of admission to the Union)

Kennedy's New Frontier

At the Democratic Party's national convention held in Los Angeles in July 1960, presidential nominee John F. Kennedy perpetuated the frontier myth with his famous "New Frontier" acceptance speech, reprinted in Vital Speeches of the Day. *Kennedy implied that the challenges of the New Frontier existed in part because of the closing of the historical frontier.*

"For I stand tonight facing west on what was once the last frontier. From the lands that stretch 3,000 miles behind me, the pioneers of old gave up their safety, their comfort and sometimes their lives to build a new world here in the West. . . .

Today some would say that those struggles are all over—that all the horizons have been explored—that all the battles have been won—that there is no longer an American frontier.

But I trust that no one in this vast assemblage will agree with those sentiments. For the problems are not all solved and the battles are not all won—and we stand today on the edge of a new frontier—the frontier of the 1960's—a frontier of unknown opportunities and perils—a frontier of unfulfilled hopes and threats.

. . . [T]he New Frontier of which I speak is not a set of promises—it is a set of challenges. It sums up not what I intend to offer the American people, but what I intend to ask of them. It appeals to their pride, not their pocketbook—it holds out the promise of more sacrifice instead of more security.

But I tell you the New Frontier is here, whether we seek it or not. Beyond that frontier are uncharted areas of science and space, unsolved problems of peace and war, unconquered pockets of ignorance and prejudice, unanswered questions of poverty and surplus.

It would be easier to shrink back from that frontier, to look to the safe mediocrity of the past, to be lulled by good intentions and high rhetoric,—and those who prefer that course should not cast their votes for me, regardless of party.

But I believe the times demand invention, innovation, imagination, decision. I am asking each of you to be new pioneers on that New Frontier."

Prescott Webb observed in an essay published in *Harper's Magazine* that Turner's paper "altered the whole course of American historical scholarship, and it is recognized as the most significant single piece of historical writing ever done in the United States."[47]

The Myth of the Frontier

Although no geographic frontier has existed in the United States for more than a century, the frontier remains a significant cultural influence on American society. The frontier influences art, popular culture, even politics. The frontier, or western, story form first popularized by James Fenimore Cooper in the early 1800s has grown into one of America's most unique and best-loved art forms. Western stories have been adapted to radio, movies, and television through the years. With stories about real or fictional characters, westerns have dramatized the broad movements of history, such as the struggle between settlers and Native Americans, as well as specific historical events such as the battle at the Alamo, or Custer's defeat at the Little Big Horn.

While scholars quibble over its influence, the settlement of the American west remains a vivid topic in popular culture, both in the United States and in Europe. Numerous scholars have studied the western to understand why it remains popular. Writing about the western novel, author James K. Folsom observes that because westerns depict the Great West, they distinguish "Americans . . . from other peoples; and the settlement of the Great West is what tells the American most about himself."[48]

Notes

Chapter 1: Europe's Frontier

1. Ray Allen Billington, *Westward Expansion: A History of the American Frontier*, 3rd. ed. New York: Macmillan, 1967, p. 21.

2. Quoted in William T. Davis, ed., William Bradford, *Bradford's History of Plymouth Plantations, 1606–1648*, 19 vols. New York: Charles Scribner's Sons, 1908, p. 146.

3. Quoted in Teresa O'Neill, ed., *Puritanism: Opposing Viewpoints*. San Diego: Greenhaven Press, 1994, p. 36.

4. John Winthrop, quoted in *Puritanism*, p. 38.

5. Quoted in *Puritanism*, pp. 36–38.

6. Billington, *Westward Expansion*, p. 72.

Chapter 2: Creating a People and a Country

7. Quoted in Henry Steel Commager, ed., *Documents of American History,* 7th ed. New York: Appleton-Century-Crofts, 1963, pp. 48–49.

8. Quoted in Commager, *Documents of American History,* pp. 48–49.

9. Quoted in "On the Desirability of Closing the Frontier," in Mortimer J. Adler, ed., *The Annals of America*, vol. 2. Chicago: Encyclopaedia Britannica, Inc., 1963, p. 208.

10. Quoted in Adler, *The Annals of America*, vol. 2, p. 209.

11. Quoted in Commager, *Documents of American History,* pp. 117–18.

Chapter 3: Unifying a Nation

12. Quoted in Commager, *Documents of American History,* p. 11.

13. Quoted in Commager, *Documents of American History,* p. 121.

14. Quoted in Commager, *Documents of American History,* pp. 123–24.

15. Quoted in Commager, *Documents of American History,* p. 189.

16. Quoted in Commager, *Documents of American History,* p. 207.

17. Quoted in Commager, *Documents of American History,* p. 207.

Chapter 4: Taming the Frontier

18. Quoted in "Backwoodsmen," in Mortimer J. Adler, ed., *Annals of America*, vol. 5, p. 206.

19. Quoted in "People of the Woods," in Albert Bushnell, ed., *American History Told by Contemporaries,* vol. III. New York: Macmillan, 1901, p. 464.

20. Quoted in "First Message to Congress, in Adler, *Annals of America*, vol. 5, p. 335.

21. Quoted in "First Message to Congress," in Adler, *Annals of America*, vol. 5, p. 336.

22. Alexis de Tocqueville, *Democracy in America,* edited and abridged by Richard D. Heffner. New York: Mentor Books, 1956, pp. 112, 114.

Chapter 5: Manifest Destiny

23. Quoted in Reginald Horsman, *Race and Manifest Destiny: The Origins of American Racial Anglo-Saxonism.* Cambridge, MA: Harvard University Press, 1981, p. 121.

24. Quoted in Ray Allen Billington, *America's Frontier Heritage.* New York: Holt, Rinehart and Winston, 1966, p. 202.

25. Quoted in Commager, *Documents of American History,* p. 308.

26. Quoted in Commager, *Documents of American History,* p. 308.

27. Quoted in Commager, *Documents of*

American History, p. 308.

28. Quoted in Commager, *Documents of American History*, p. 308.

29. O'Sullivan's famous passage has been reproduced extensively in frontier literature. This quotation is taken from Albert K. Weinberg, *Manifest Destiny: A Study of Nationalist Expansionism in American History*. Gloucester, MA: Peter Smith, 1958, p. 112.

30. Quoted in Commager, *Documents of American History*, p. 311.

31. Quoted in Commager, *Documents of American History*, pp. 308–309.

Chapter 6: Transforming the West

32. Although this famous aphorism is almost always attributed to Horace Greeley, it originated in an editorial written by John L. B. Soule and published in the *Terre Haute (Indiana) Express* in 1851. "Go West, young man, go west!" Soule advised. Greeley was so impressed with the advice that he reprinted and expanded on it. These versions of Soule's and Greeley's quotes are taken from the *Home Book of Quotations Classical and Modern*, 10th ed. Burton Stevenson, ed. New York: Dodd, Meade & Co., 1967, p. 2131.

33. Quoted in Rodman Wilson Paul, *Mining Frontiers of the Far West, 1848–1880*. New York: Holt, Rinehart and Winston, 1963, p. 14.

34. Mark Twain, *Roughing It*. New York: Harper & Brothers, Publishers, 1871, pp. 169–70.

35. Billington, *Westward Expansion*, p. 661.

36. Quoted in Teresa O'Neill, ed., *The American Frontier: Opposing Viewpoints*. San Diego: Greenhaven Press, 1994, p. 196.

37. Willa Cather, *My Antonia*. Boston: Houghton Mifflin, 1954, pp. 21–22.

38. Frederick Jackson Turner, *The Frontier in American History*. New York: Henry Holt, 1920, 1948, pp. 2–3.

Chapter 7: The Frontier's Significance

39. Turner, *The Frontier in American History*, pp. 9–11.

40. Turner, *The Frontier in American History*, p. 12.

41. Turner, *The Frontier in American History*, p. 30.

42. Turner, *The Frontier in American History*, p. 32.

43. Turner, *The Frontier in American History*, p. 37.

44. Turner, *The Frontier in American History*, p. 38.

45. Turner, *The Frontier in American History*. p. 38

46. Billington, *Westward Expansion*, p. 757.

47. Walter Prescott Webb, "Ended: 400 Year Boom, Reflections on the Age of the Frontier," *Harper's Magazine*, October 1951, p. 27.

48. James K. Folsom, *The American Western Novel*. New Haven, CT: College & University Press, 1966, pp. 29–30.

For Further Reading

Sue R. Brandt, *Facts About the Fifty States.* Second Revised Edition. New York: Franklin Watts, 1988. This overview includes history, geography, and trivia about the nation's fifty states.

Bronwyn Mills, *The Mexican War.* New York: Facts On File, 1992. A detailed look at the U.S. conflict with Mexico for the territories in the American Southwest. For older readers.

Richard B. Morris, *The War of 1812.* Minneapolis, MN: Lerner Publications, 1985. A good overview of the War of 1812, for younger readers.

Diana Reische, *Founding the American Colonies.* New York: Franklin Watts, 1989. Somewhat traditional retelling of the founding of England's American colonies.

John Anthony Scott, *Settlers on the Eastern Shore, 1607–1750.* New York: Facts On File, 1991. Interprets the colonial period of America through historical figures. For older readers.

———, *The Story of America.* Washington, DC: The National Geographic Society, 1984. Excellent overview of American history filled with period art, historical photographs, and photographs of arti-facts. Contains chapters on the opening and closing of the west.

Edwin Tunis, *Frontier Living.* New York: Thomas Y. Crowell, 1961. A pictorial history of life on the colonial frontier.

Laura Ingalls Wilder, *Little House in the Big Woods.* New York: Harper & Row, 1971. Set in the Big Woods of Wisconsin, this is the first of a series of books that expertly captures the daily pioneer experience in the American Midwest. The series follows the saga of the Ingalls family as father Charles Ingalls moves from homestead to homestead in search of a better life for his family. In chronological order the other titles in the series are: *Little House on the Prairie, On the Banks of Plum Creek, By the Shores of Silver Lake, Little Town on the Prairie, These Happy Golden Years,* and *The First Four Years.*

Donald Zochert, *Laura: The Life of Laura Ingalls Wilder.* Chicago: Henry Regnery, 1976. This biography of Laura Ingalls Wilder, creator of the famous "Little House" books, fills in the gaps of the celebrated author's early years and her adult life. Wilder is a junior version of Willa Cather.

Works Consulted

Periodicals

Walter Prescott Webb, "Ended: 400 Year Boom, Reflections on the Age of the Frontier," *Harper's Magazine*, October 1951. Reviews Frederick Jackson Turner's frontier hypothesis, its effect on the study of history, and the adoption of the frontier as a metaphor in American culture.

——, "Windfalls of the Frontier," *Harper's Magazine*, November 1951. Examines some of the legacy of the American frontier.

Books

Mortimer J. Adler, ed., *The Annals of America*. 20 vols. Chicago: Encyclopaedia Brittannica, Inc. 1968–1974.

The American Heritage Pictorial Atlas of United States History. New York: American Heritage Publishing Co., 1966. Although its maps are extremely helpful in following the frontier west, the text in this pictorial history is too brief and superficial to adequately support them.

Ray Allen Billington, *America's Frontier Heritage*. New York: Holt, Rinehart and Winston, 1966. This scholarly study of the legacy of the American frontier supports Turner's hypothesis with a myriad of data.

——, *Westward Expansion: A History of the American Frontier*. 3rd. ed. New York: Macmillan, 1967. In this exhaustive history of the advancement of the American frontier, Billington fleshes out the frontier hypothesis as he imagines Turner himself would have.

Albert Bushnell, ed., *American History Told by Contemporaries*. 15 vols. New York: Macmillan, 1901. First-person accounts of frontier life.

Kenneth Carley, *The Sioux Uprising of 1862*. St. Paul, MN: The Minnesota Historical Society, 1976. A brief, objective, and readable history of the Dakota War of 1862, written before the adoption of today's politically sensitive language.

Willa Cather, *My Antonia*. Boston: Houghton Mifflin, 1954. A fictional treatment of the settling of the Nebraska Great Plains by American and European immigrants in the 1880s. One of the definitive pioneer novels, *My Antonia* is still a reading pleasure three-quarters of a century after its publication.

Henry Steel Commager, ed., *Documents of American History*. 7th ed. New York: Appleton-Century-Crofts, 1963. A convenient anthology of significant documents in American history, with a strong emphasis on legislation and other important documents responding to frontier needs.

James Fenimore Cooper, *The Deerslayer*. Boston and New York: Houghton, Mifflin, 1898. First in the chronology of the *Leatherstocking Tales*, this installment was among the last of the series to be written.

Bernard DeVoto, *Across the Wide Missouri*. Boston: Houghton Mifflin, 1947. Lively, interpretive account of the fur-trading era in the American west.

John Filson, *The Life and Adventures of Colonel Daniel Boon, The First White Settler of the State of Kentucky*. Brooklyn, NY: Printed for C. Wilder, 1823. Although authorship was credited to Daniel Boone, schoolteacher and land speculator John Filson actually wrote this colorful and error-filled account of Boone's life as part of *The Discovery, Settlement and Present State of Kentucke*, a promotional volume compiled to interest Americans in Kentucky. This account of Boone's life turned the frontiersman into the nation's first western hero, and set the standard for heroes for the next two centuries.

James K. Folsom, *The American Western Novel*. New Haven, CT: College & University Press, 1966. A scholarly study of the western novel as an American art form.

Reginald Horsman, *Race and Manifest Destiny: The Origins of American Racial Anglo-Saxonism*. Cambridge, MA: Harvard University Press, 1981. An examination of the connections between manifest destiny and America's racial attitudes.

J. Franklin Jameson, ed. *Original Narratives of Early American History*. 19 vols. New York: Charles Scribner's Sons, 1908. First-person accounts of life in the colonies in the first half of the seventeenth century.

Alvin M. Josephy Jr. et al., *War on the Frontier*. Alexandria, VA: Time-Life Books, 1986. A pictorial history of the role of the frontier in the Civil War.

Paul O'Neill, *The Frontiersmen*. Alexandria, VA: Time-Life Books, 1977. An entertaining account of the American frontier from the age of exploration to the revolutionary period.

Teresa O'Neill, ed., *The American Frontier: Opposing Viewpoints*. San Diego: Greenhaven Press, 1994. Covers a wide variety of topics through frontier history. Viewpoints are not always as opposing as the title suggests.

———, *Puritanism: Opposing Viewpoints*. San Diego: Greenhaven Press, 1994. First-person essay that provides a good example of Puritan attitudes in the early 1600s.

Ernest Staples Osgood, ed., *The Field Notes of Captain William Clark*. New Haven, CT and London: Yale University Press, 1964. This volume offers facsimiles and annotated printed text of pages from famous explorer William Clark's field notes. The notes were discovered in a St. Paul, Minnesota, attic in 1953. How they got there remains a mystery.

Rodman Wilson Paul, *Mining Frontiers of the Far West, 1848–1880*. New York: Holt, Rinehart and Winston, 1963. A scholarly study of America's famous mining frontiers, which helped to open the American west.

John Steinbeck, *The Red Pony*. New York: Bantam Books, 1948. One of the most beloved of Steinbeck's early novels, set in the early 1900s. Grandfather's poignant speech at the novel's conclusion captures the sense of loss many felt when the frontier era ended.

Francis Newton Thorpe, ed., *The Statesmanship of Andrew Jackson as Told in His Writings and Speeches*. New York: The Tandy-Thomas Company, 1909. Jackson's own frontier attitudes and his influence on the nation as a frontier president are presented in his own words.

Alexis de Tocqueville, *Democracy in America*. Edited and abridged by Richard D. Heffner. New York: Mentor Books, 1956. Originally published in 1835, this book remains one of the most comprehensive examinations of American democracy, cultural institutions, and uniqueness. Its direct references to the frontier are few, but the origins of many American traits are identified.

Mark Twain, *Roughing It*. New York: Harper & Brothers, Publishers, 1871. Twain takes on the American west in this early work.

Frederick Jackson Turner, *The Frontier in American History*. New York: Henry Holt, 1920, 1948. This anthology of Turner's frontier writings includes his landmark essay "The Significance of the Frontier in American History," which introduced his frontier hypothesis.

Lyon Gardiner Tyler, *Narratives of Early Virginia, 1606–1625*. New York: Charles Scribner's Sons, 1907. This volume includes *Descriptions of Virginia and Proceedings of the Colonie by Captain John Smith, 1612*. Narrative by one of America's early citizens offers a glimpse into life in America during the age of exploration.

Albert K. Weinberg, *Manifest Destiny: A Study of Nationalist Expansionism in American History*. Gloucester, MA: Peter Smith, 1958. A scholarly study of the mind-set that pushed American boundaries to the Pacific in the nineteenth century.

Speeches

John F. Kennedy, acceptance address delivered at the Democratic National Convention, Los Angeles, California, July 15, 1960, in *Vital Speeches of the Day*, August 1, 1960, pp. 610–12. In this speech, Kennedy outlined the New Frontier, which later defined his presidency.

Index

Picture Credits

Cover photo: Stock Montage, Inc.

The Bettmann Archive, 15, 49, 90

Library of Congress, 11 13 (both), 14, 17, 19, 21, 25, 29, 31, 33, 39, 41, 45, 46, 48, 52, 55, 56 (top), 65 (both), 66, 69, 72, 78, 79, 81, 82 (right), 88, 94

National Archives, 9, 92

North Wind Picture Archives, 23

Stock Montage, Inc., 40

Woolaroc Museum, 56 (bottom)

About the Author

Roger Barr is a writer and publisher who lives in St. Paul, Minnesota. He has written widely on historical, political, business, and social topics. His novel *The Treasure Hunt* was published by Medallion Press in 1992. He has written five previous books for Lucent: *The Vietnam War, The Importance of Richard Nixon, The Importance of Malcolm X, Radios: Wireless Sound,* and *Cities.*